A DEFENCE OF ANARCHIST COMMUNISM

by Brian Morris

This first edition
printed 2022

Published by
Freedom Press
84b Whitechapel High
St, London
E1 7QX
freedompress.org.uk

ISBN
978-1-904491-39-2

CONTENTS

Introduction

For more than 40 years I have been defending through pamphlets, articles and books, as well as letters (to *Freedom* and *Green Anarchist*) the integrity, importance and contemporary relevance of anarchist communism as a historical movement and as a political tradition. Drawing on my earlier writings this short book offers an introduction to anarchist communism – otherwise known as libertarian socialism or social anarchism – both as a political philosophy and as a revolutionary praxis. The book essentially consists of four parts.

In the first part (Section One) I specifically address the question "what is anarchist communism?" I give an account of its emergence as a historical movement and as a distinct political tradition within the wider context of anarchist politics. I outline the four basic principles or tenets of anarchist communism, as expressed by the earlier anarchist communists such as Peter Kropotkin and Errico Malatesta[1]. These tenets are: a critique and opposition to the state and all

---

1   Kropotkin (1842-1921) was a Russian former prince who is broadly considered to be the founding father of anarchist communist theory. Malatesta (1853-1932) was a key Italian theorist and direct actionist.

forms of hierarchy and oppressive authority; a fervent anti-capitalism; a vision of a free society based on mutual aid, voluntary associations and self-managed communities; and finally, the "grounding" of its politics in a philosophy of evolutionary naturalism.

In the second part (chapters two and three) I discuss various radical political movements that have contemporary relevance, in terms of which anarchist communism has tended to be defined. I am not concerned in this book with those political traditions that dominate contemporary world politics, for example fascism, neo-conservatism (and its offspring, autocratic populism), theocracy and the various forms of liberal democracy. All these traditions support a capitalist economy and uphold structures of political domination via state power. I focus instead on these radical traditions which, like anarchist communism, challenge to varying degrees global capitalism and the hegemony of the nation-state. I therefore discuss, with a degree of sympathy, six contemporary forms of radical politics, namely Max Stirner's egoism[2], individualist anarchism (mutualism), Marxism and religious anarchism, along with two radical tendencies that have only emerged in recent decades.

---

2   See page 20.

These are anarcho-primitivism and post (modern) anarchism. I specifically discuss the "ethos" or ideology of postmodernism and stress that "post" anarchism is largely a revamping of Max Stirner's egoistic insurrectionism, essentially a hark back to the early nineteenth century.

What then emerges from my discussion is that anarchist communism in terms of politics rejects primitivism, Stirner's egoism, the market economy and the Marxist "statist" conception of radical politics. In terms of its metaphysics[3], as evolutionary naturalism – and thus pro-science – anarchist communism rejects all forms of religious mysticism as well as postmodern nihilism.

With respect to each of these radical traditions, I offer critiques from an anarchist communist perspective, highlighting their tendency to misrepresent libertarian socialism, whilst indicating the limitations of each tradition.

In the third part of the book (Section Four) I address what has been widely described as the "post-structuralist" critique of anarchism – although by the word anarchism scholars invariably mean the anarchist communism of Mikhail Bakunin[4], Kropotkin and Malatesta.

---

3   The "first principles" of a concept.
4   Bakunin (1814-76) was most famous for clashing with Marx in the First International. He noted that "liberty without socialism is privilege, injustice; socialism without liberty is slavery and brutality."

However, hardly any of the so-called post-structuralist philosophers, French or otherwise, very seriously engage in their own writings with anarchist communism, either as a historical social movement or as a political philosophy and praxis,

Their so-called "critique" is rather that of a coterie of academic theorists, drawing on the writings of a rather select number of post-structuralist philosophers – mainly Jacques Lacan, Jean-François Lyotard, Jacques Derrida, Michel Foucault and Gilles Deleuze – to rebuke an earlier generation of anarchist communists for their philosophical and political naivety.

Anarchist communists are thus criticised, for example, for viewing power only as coercive and repressive; for having a Cartesian[5] or essentialist conception of human subjectivity and for living in a "fantasy world," believing that a social revolution is not only possible but imminent. These critiques by post (modern) anarchists (as they describe themselves), as I emphasise, reflect a warped understanding, even an outright misrepresentation, of anarchist communist writings on power, the human subject and social revolution.

---

5   After the philosopher Descartes, who argued that matter consists of three parts, matter, mind and God. He separated the experience of the body from the deductive reasoning of the mind.

In Section Four I therefore take the opportunity to detail what these concepts mean for anarchist communists. I indicate their complex understanding of power relations in society (they certainly never dreamed of "abolishing" power); their equally complex understanding of the human subject, recognising that humans are biological and social beings as well as unique individuals; and finally, the anarchist communist understanding of a social revolution. Contrary to what post-anarchists imply, this certainly did not entail establishing new forms of political sovereignty, nor did a social revolution imply a sudden apocalyptical event. For anarchist communists recognised that a better world, a free society, would be a gradual process, as the writings of Malatesta and Rudolf Rocker[6] attest, involving long and protracted class struggles.

In opposing the parliamentary road to socialism, which they felt would only lead to liberal reforms, and the Marxist conception of a disciplined party which would through state power enact "the dictatorship of the proletariat", anarchist communists rejected what they termed "political action" – essentially any political activity involving the state.

---

6   Rocker (1873-1958) was a leading figure in the European anarcho-syndicalist movement of political trade unionism.

In contrast, anarchist communism extols "direct action" and in the fourth and final part of the book (Section Five) I discuss at length the four main political strategies adopted by anarchist communists in their efforts to invoke a social revolution – that is, the radical transformation of capitalism and the existing political landscape. These are insurrectionism, anarcho-syndicalism, libertarian politics and community activism.

Although there has been a tendency for some radical activists and political theorists to set up a completely facile dichotomy between insurrectionism (supposedly some new phenomenon) and old-fashioned anarchist communism, I emphasise that insurrectionism – protests, strikes and demonstrations, or what Kropotkin describes as "the spirit of revolt" – has always been an important political strategy and an intrinsic part of anarchist communism. Indeed, I emphasise that insurrectionism, specifically protests and demonstrations against global capitalism, has always been a key strategy of anarchist communists – past and present.

Likewise, anarcho-syndicalism (or class struggle anarchism) has always been an important political strategy for anarchist communists. Again, the tendency of some political theorists to set up a radical dichotomy between anarcho-syndicalism (a strategy) and anarchist communism (a political philosophy) is completely misconceived. For virtually all the early anarchist communists – Kropotkin, Malatesta, Emma Goldman[7] and Rocker – were firm advocates of anarcho-syndicalism as a political praxis. This strategy entails an emphasis on the role of trade unions and workers' associations in both defending the rights, wages and living conditions of workers within the existing capitalist system, and in "re-constructing" social life through direct action, workers' solidarity and the creation of a federation of rural and industrial workers' unions – free, integral and self-managed. Trade unions are thus viewed as having a dual function in defending workers' interests within capitalism, and through class struggle forming the "embryo" of a future socialist society – or what Kropotkin describes as "free communism".

In contrast to anarcho-syndicalism, libertarian politics, as a political strategy, puts a focal emphasis on politics rather than on economics, and on the community, whether neighbourhoods within a city or the local municipality. It seeks through direct action to create a confederal system of decentralised municipalities, each municipality managing its own affairs through a local assembly, and forms of direct democracy. As an example of

---

7   Goldman (1868-1940) is regarded as one of the most important anarchist theoreticians of the 19th and early 20th century, and was an influential speaker on social issues particularly in the US.

this political strategy I focus specifically on Murray Bookchin's[8] theory of libertarian municipalism. Significantly Bookchin makes a clear and important distinction between politics – the ways in which people organise their everyday social life – and statecraft, which is focused on the state as a form of government that upholds class exploitation.

In the final pages of Section Five I discuss the political strategy of community activism. This encapsulates what Kropotkin meant when he implored people to "act for yourselves": a strategy that Colin Ward[9] describes as "anarchy in action". Community activism involves a wide variety of "direct actions" independent of both the state and capitalism. These may entail squatting or establishing a local housing association, the creation of food co-ops or independent free schools[10], or simply organising campaigns around specific environmental or community issues.

---

8   Bookchin (1921-2006) was a famed theorist in the latter half of the 20th century. An originator of the radical theory of social ecology, his work also spans urban planning and post-scarcity (theorising how a future society which sustainably produces enough for everyone might function).

9   Ward (1924-2010), a long-time member of and writer for Freedom Press, was probably the best-known British anarchist writer of his generation. Particularly well known through his work on housing policy and childhood under capitalism, he was a strong proponent of "everyday" anarchism, exploring how humans naturally act in anarchistic ways when left uninterfered with by the pressures of state and capital.

10   Not to be confused with Conservative hijacking of the term. Anarchist free schools derive from the thinking of Francisco Ferrer in the early 1900s, emphasising self-directed development, horizontal learning practices and a de-emphasis on bureaucracy in the learning process.

I stress in this section that for anarchist communists all four political strategies are closely interlinked, that a plurality of strategies and tactics may be employed, and that no contradiction is envisaged among anarchist communists between engaging in insurrectionism and class struggle, and creating alternative forms of social life based on mutual and voluntary associations.

I conclude the book with a short epilogue, offering a few final reflections on anarchist communism as a distinct but living tradition. I stress that in an era when global capitalism reigns virtually triumphant, creating conditions of political turmoil and social dislocation, and severe ecological problems, including that of global warming, we surely need to take seriously the political legacy of anarchist communism given that all other contemporary political traditions – liberal democracy, neoliberalism, Marxism and theocracy (religious fundamentalism) – are now morally and politically bankrupt.

Acknowledgements

I first discovered anarchism at the age of 29 when quite by chance I met Bill Gate. It was at a meeting on comprehensive education at Conway Hall in London. Bill was an affable working-class bloke, rather large and Bakunin-like, and he introduced me to what was, for me then, a rather esoteric political tradition, namely anarchism. Ever since I have considered myself an anarchist; that is, a libertarian socialist. I have always been grateful to Bill Gate for this introduction.

The present book has its origins in a talk I gave on contemporary anarchism to the Anarchist Communist Group in London in April 2018.

I am grateful to Bonnie Vandesteeg and Nick Heath for their invitation and encouragement over many years. Finally, I am grateful to my friend Angela Travis for typing my manuscript and for her long support.

Glossary

Anarchism, a political philosophy and movement that rejects coercive hierarchies and illegitimate authority in favour of a society based on direct democracy, voluntary association, and the common ownership of property, goods and services. As such anarchists call for the abolition of the state, capitalism and private property as they are irreconcilable with anarchism's core principles.

Bourgeoisie, in Marxist theory the class which owns the means of production, capital, and is placed at the top of the economic herirarchy in capitalist society. Concerned with the protection of private property and other means of maintaining their class interests.

Capitalism, a global economic system based on the accumulation of profit through the exploitation of wage labour and the private ownership of property and the means of production.

Class, a socially and economically defined section of people in capitalism, delineated by their relationship with the means of production. Classes have distinct interests, producing class conflict.

Collectivism, a form of social organisation and political philosophy where the well-being of the group is prioritised over that of the individual. Often contrasted, although not mutually exclusive, with *individualism*.

Communism, a political philosophy which advocates for a stateless society without social class, money or private property. The means of production and their produce are held in common and equitably distributed through society as needed. Sometimes used interchangeably with socialism.

Enlightenment, a philosophical movement that emerged in Europe in the 17th and 18th centuries. Focusing on the ideas of scientific reason and human happiness, it is seen as the forerunner to the philosophies of *liberalism*, *socialism*, *anarchism*, *individualism*, and *communism*.

Epistemology, the study of knowledge. A major branch of philosophy, epistemology encompasses the limatestion of knowledge, what it means to know something and so on.

Humanism, a philosophical and moral stance that seeks to interpret existence and the world around by centering human experience. Humanists generally advocate on behalf of all humanity for individual dignity, personal freedoms and human rights.

Individualism, a political and moral philosophy that prioritises an individual's freedoms, personal autonomy and self interest. Often contrasted, although not mutually exclusive, with *collectivism*.

Liberalism, the dominant strain of political thought for more than 200 years. Liberalism is a flexible ideology dedicated to the preservation of private property and capitalist exploitation.

Marxism, the political, social and economic theories of Karl Marx. Marx advocated for workers' revolution and the abolition of Capitalism in favour of Communism, although there are many different interpretations of his works.

Mutual aid, a theory of organisation based on voluntary cooperation, solidarity and collective participation in response to a common struggle.

Nihilism, a philosophy that rejects traditional morality and values as meaningless and questions whether human existence has any intrinsic meaning.

Postmodernism, an intellectual, social and cultural movement interested in interrogating the so-called 'grand narratives' of modernity. Postmodernists are concerned with the operation of ideology in maintaining power in society.

Praxis, a form of political activity featuring the interaction between theory and action, both grounding theory in material conditions and, in turn, using it to act upon the world to secure revolutionary change.

Property, a state enforced legal concept within capitalist society denoting the ownership of land and the means of production by private interests.

State, The, the institutions of the elite, a tool with which the minority ruling class centralises and maintains its hold on power through coercion and a monopoly on violence. Anarchists oppose the state as its centralised and coercive nature is incompatible with anarchism, further rejecting taking control of its institutions as this would only replace one group of rulers with another.

Socialism, a left wing philosophy encompassing various economic, political and social models generally characterised by the shared advocacy of common ownership and collective organisation.

A Defence of
Anarchist-Communism

AROUND 2002, at the age of 81, the social ecologist Murray Bookchin suddenly announced that he had ceased to define himself as an anarchist, leading Ian McKay (2007)[11] to suggest that Bookchin in his last years attempted to "trash his own legacy". Nothing could be further from the truth. For in his last years, under the rubric of "communalism", Bookchin in fact reaffirmed his commitment to the kind of "libertarian socialism" that he had advocated all his life, and which in the past he had variously described as either anarcho-communism or social anarchism.

What Bookchin then meant by "anarchism" was the "post-left anarchy" that had become popular in the United States, and was equivalent to what he had earlier critiqued, in a highly polemical tract, as "lifestyle anarchism" (1995). It was, according to Bookchin, comprised specifically of five strands of contemporary radical thought. These were, namely; petty-bourgeois Stirnerite egoism (Jason McQuinn); the anarcho-primitivism of John Zerzan[12] (1994)

---

11   McKay is a prolific collator and editor of anarchist texts, most notably as lead author of *The Anarchist FAQ*.
12   While his work has largely fallen out of vogue in the 2020s, Zerzan's writing was an inspirational factor for many around eco direct action groups such as Earth First!

with its anti-civilization rhetoric; the Nietzschean aesthetic individualism of Hakim Bey (1991)[13] and his advocacy of the "poetic terrorism"; the reactionary romanticism of the crypto fascist and spiritualist Rudolf Bahro who yearned for a Green Adolf, and, finally, the individualistic tendencies that Bookchin discerned in the writings not only of Emma Goldman but of the existentialist Susan Brown (1993).

Anarchism, for Bookchin, thus came to mean "post-leftist" anarchism; the kind of anarchism that completely repudiates the socialist legacy of the nineteenth century libertarian socialists, prototypically identified with the radical politics of Michael Bakunin and Peter Kropotkin. Indeed Bookchin was simply reflecting the "chasm" that had already been created by the egoists and radical primitivists themselves in their highly dismissive attitude towards not only the Enlightenment and civilization but to the socialism that was intrinsic to so-called "classical" anarchism – the libertarian socialism of Bakunin, Kropotkin, Goldman, Malatesta, Gustav Landauer[14] and Rocker, otherwise known as revolutionary socialism or simply anarcho-communism.

---

13   Peter Lamborn Wilson's most famous work is *Temporary Autonomous Zones*, which was well received by the free party, rave and occupation scenes in the '90s and '00s. He was subsequently disgraced when his links to the US childlove movement became widely known.
14   Landauer (1870-1919) was a leading German anarchist and pacifist, killed during the German revolution of 1918-19.

In his last years Bookchin therefore came to describe four contemporary radical traditions; anarchism (as described above), revolutionary syndicalism, Marxism and his own brand of libertarian socialism – communalism (Bookchin 2007).

Consonant with earlier forms of anarchist communism, Bookchin expressed his commitment to its four basic tenets. These are:

> "... a confederation of decentralised municipalities; an unwavering opposition to statism; a belief in direct democracy and a vision of a libertarian communist society"
> (1995 B: 60 – see Bibliography pages 135-142).

In his last years Bookchin envisaged an ecological society that was libertarian, socialist and democratic.

Quite misleadingly, however, Bookchin identifies anarchism as the "post-left" radicalism of the anarcho-primitivists and the devotees of Stirner and Nietzsche, while radically separateating anarcho-syndicalism from his own libertarian socialism. Both of these moves are problematic to say the least.

There is now an absolute welter of books on anarchism – on its philosophy, its politics and its history, and there are many biographies on some of the key figures in anarchism as a political movement.[15] How different from when in February 1966 I first visited Freedom Bookshop in London, and eagerly gathered some pamphlets – not much else was available then – on and by Bakunin, Kropotkin and Goldman.

Leaving aside Bookchin's own narrow and highly idiosyncratic definition, anarchism as a political tradition has been described in two very distinct ways, both of which have validity. On the one hand anarchism has been described as a broad current of political thought going back to ancient times, to Lao Tzu in China and the Buddha in India.[16] It thus incorporates any person, movement (religious or otherwise), or social philosophy that has expressed libertarian sentiments, or in some sense opposed the state and all forms of coercive authority (Marshall 1992: 53-107).

Contrary to what post(modern) anarchists often imply, in the past not all revolts and acts of insurrection can be viewed as either progressive or libertarian: for the outcome was often the re-affirmation of other forms of authority; specifically what the sociologist Max Weber

15   **Morris note**: Noteworthy examples, among many, are Benjamin Frank's Rebel Alliances (2006) on contemporary British anarchism; David Berry's (2009) history of the French anarchist movement, and David Turcato's (2015) account of Errico Malatesta's experiments with revolutionary politics between 1889 and 1900.

16   **Morris note**: In fact, in 1981, some 20 years before John Rapp's (2012) important and seminal study of Daoism, I wrote an essay specifically on Lao Tzu (Zi) and Anarchism (Morris 1996: 37-52).

6

described as charismatic authority. This is a form of theocracy. Insurrectionism or "revolt" cannot be equated with anarchism or with a libertarian sensibility.

But around 1900 a German academic lawyer, Paul Eltzbacher, wrote a book which met with Kropotkin's approval, outlining the political philosophies of seven "exponents" of anarchism. They have come to be known as the "seven sages of anarchism" for all were fundamentally opposed to the modern state (Van der Walt and Schmidt 2009: 36).

They include: the eighteenth century English utilitarian philosopher William Godwin; Pierre-Joseph Proudhon, a libertarian French socialist who envisaged a form of "market socialism"; Benjamin Tucker, an American individualist anarchist, a follower of Proudhon and Josiah Warren; the German schoolteacher Max Stirner, who in the early nineteenth century extolled the virtues of an extreme form of individualism; Leo Tolstoy, the famous Russian novelist who advocated a form of religious anarchism, and, finally, two Russian libertarian socialists, both from aristocratic backgrounds, Michael Bakunin and Peter Kropotkin.

What is remarkable is that when there was a resurgence of anarchism in the 1960s most of the anthologies of anarchist writings produced in that decade (e.g. Horowitz 1964, Shatz 1971), as well as George Woodcock's (1962) classic history of anarchism, tended to adopt Eltzbacher's conceptual framework and thus describe several distinct "types" or "currents" of anarchism – the key criteria linking them being their opposition to the state. The types indicated include, specifically, religious, anarcho-syndicalist, individualist and communist forms of anarchism.

But with the publication of Peter Marshall's book *Demanding the Impossible* (1992) subtitled a "history of anarchism", some 30 years later, anarchism was further widened to include anyone who expresses in any way libertarian sentiments, or who even pretends to be anti-state. Although an excellent text in many ways, well-researched, lucidly written and engaging, Marshall expresses in the book a marked antipathy towards Bookchin's libertarian socialism, viewing the social ecologist as akin to Lenin in his sectarian politics (though Bookchin is no more sectarian than the Stirnerite egoists and the anarcho-primitivists in their opposition to socialism – indeed in being "enemies" (no less) of society (S. E. Parker et al 2011) Marshall contends that Bookchin's critique of "lifestyle anarchism" is "muddled and absurd" (1992 (2008): 694). Marshall, however, completely misjudges Bookchin's critique of "post-left" anarchy. Bookchin expresses a fervent opposition, a "chasm" as he rhetorically put it, between libertarian socialism and all forms of what he envisaged as "bourgeois" individualism – as well as opposing, equally fervently, statism and capitalism. He was not suggesting an opposition between libertarian politics and socialism, which he felt, like Bakunin, were inextricably linked. In fact, Bakunin extolled the libertarian aspects of an earlier generation of libertarian socialists (anarchist communists).

But in his history of anarchism, Marshall includes many people who are not by any stretch of the imagination, anarchists. They include, for example, Jean-Jacques Rousseau, who, by Marshall's own admission, was an advocate of the corporate state with totalitarian implications; Margaret Thatcher along with her guru Ayn Rand, who were both student advocates of free market capitalism and the minimal (but highly coercive) state; and the authoritarian Marxist Che Guevara (1992: 516-18, 559-62), as well as many other figures whose status as anarchists is at least debatable, and certainly marginal to anarchism as a political movement.

But the fact is that anarchism has been viewed simply as an "anti-authoritarian impulse" which embraces a bewildering variety of historical figures who have been described as anarchists, besides the anarchist communists like Bakunin and Kropotkin. They include, for example, Herbert Spencer, Mohandas Gandhi, Nicolas Berdyaev,

Murray Rothbard, Leo Tolstoy, Max Stirner, Ayn Rand and Friedrich Nietzsche. This has led many scholars, especially Marxists, to dismiss anarchism as a completely incoherent political philosophy (e.g. Molyneaux 2011:10).

This is certainly not the case, for there is another way of describing anarchism as a political tradition, and that is to recognise that anarchism is fundamentally a historical social movement and political philosophy that emerged around 1870, mainly among working-class members of the International Working Men's Association, widely known as the First International. It involved a "split" or a "great schism" – as James Joll (1964: 84-114) called it – within the association. It is usually described as if it focused around a personal dispute between Marx and Bakunin. But as G. D. H. Cole (1954: 88-133) and others have suggested, this schism wasn't simply a clash of personalities, but involved two factions within the socialist movement, and two quite different conceptions of socialism, of the processes of social transformation – revolutionary change – and the conditions of human emancipation. The anarchist faction did not originally describe themselves as anarchists but rather as "federalists" or as "anti-authoritarian socialists", but they came to adopt the label of their Marxist opponents, and described themselves as "anarchist communists".

As a political movement and tradition anarchist communism thus emerged among the workers of Spain, France, Italy and Switzerland in the aftermath of the Paris Commune. It had its iconic founding at an international congress of anarchists at St. Imier in Switzerland in September 1872 (Morris 2018: 231-34).

Among the more well-known proponents of anarchist communism were Elisee Reclus, James Guillaume, Enrico Malatesta, Carlo Cafiero, Jean Grave and Kropotkin. Louise Michel[17] was closely associated with the movement in France, but had been deported to New Caledonia after the defeat of the Paris Commune. She spent six years in exile (Thomas 1980). Between 1870 and 1930 anarchism, as revolutionary/libertarian socialism, spread throughout the world and was by no means restricted to Europe. Kropotkin, who was a key theorist of anarchist communism, described it as a kind of "synthesis" between radical liberalism – libertarianism with its emphasis on the liberty of the individual – and socialism (or communism) which implied a repudiation of capitalism and all forms of coercive authority and puts an emphasis

---

17   Reclus (1830-1905) was an eminent French geographer and close comrade of Kropotkin. Cafiero (1846-92) was a key supporter of the Bakuninist wing in the First International. Grave (1854-1939) edited multiple 19th century anarchist publications including *Le Revolt*. Michel (1830-1905) was an educator, journalist and anarchist activist who became prominent during her participation in the Commune.

on communal life and voluntary associations, on equality and social solidarity. (Baldwin 1970: 53). The ethos of anarchist communism is well expressed in the famous adage of Bakunin: "That liberty without socialism is privilege and injustice and that socialism without liberty is slavery and brutality" (Lehning 1973:110).

Two points may be made here. The first is that towards the end of the nineteenth century, given the avant garde ethos that was characteristic of the period, several varieties of anarchism emerged. Nevertheless, anarchist communism seems to have been the main form of anarchism, especially among working people and trade unionists.

Secondly, the tendency of Marxists, academic philosophers, and egoists (including the post-anarchists) to set up a radial dichotomy between anarchism and socialism is quite misleading on both conceptual and historical grounds, distortsing our understanding of socialism. Anarchist communism is a form of revolutionary or libertarian socialism. It needs, therefore, to be acknowledged that "both Bakunin and Kropotkin defined anarchism as an anti-capitalist ideology and a form of socialism" (Van der Walt and Schmidt 2009: 46, Morris 2018: 231-32).[18]

---

18 **Morris note**: For an important study of the First International and the origins of the anarchist communist movement, written from an anarchist perspective see Graham 2015.

The anarchist communism that emerged as a distinct political philosophy at the end of the nineteenth century was not the creation of one iconic figure, nor was it the creation of academic scholars – it emerged from within a historical class movement. It arose out of the struggles of working people against the social oppression and the exploitative working conditions of industrial capitalism. It may be defined (below) in terms of four basic tenets, although it is worth noting at this juncture that distinction needs to be made between metaphysics, the basic ontologies that people hold regarding the nature of reality (the natural world) and the place of humans within it; specific political philosophies, such as that of egoism or anarchist communism; and the various political strategies that people may engage in, both in their struggles against the state and capitalism, and in creating alternative forms of social life through mutual aid and voluntary cooperation.

The four basic tenets or principles of anarchist communism are as follows:

First, anarchist communism entails the rejection of state power and all forms of hierarchy and oppression; it is a critique of all forms of power and authority that curtail the liberty of the individual person. For social anarchists, of course, the individual is viewed not as an abstract possessive individual, still less a fixed benign essence, but as a unique being who is both natural – for humans are earthly and social beings involved in a multiplicity of social relations, identities and social groups.[19]

In being against the state, anarchist communists are also opposed, not only to the formation of political parties and participation in parliamentary government (i.e. elections) but also against any form of Marxist "revolutionary" government or "workers" state," as well as being opposed to the ideology of the modern nation-state – namely nationalism. Anarchist communism, it is worth stressing, is a synonym of libertarian socialism, and places a crucial emphasis on freedom – the liberty of the individual person. Many anarchist communists, however, in supporting and often eagerly embracing anti-capitalist struggles and national liberation movements (such as the Zapatistas in Mexico[20]), can all too easily support authoritarian structures and hierarchy! Likewise, in emphasising that the anarchism at the end of the nineteenth century was an intrinsic part of a wider working class (socialist) movement, and

---

19   **Morris note**: For a further elaboration of the triadic ontology of the human subject, and a defence of Bakunin against his post-anarchist critics see my pamphlet and essay *Bakunin and the Human Subject* (Morris 2014C, see section 4/2).

20   The EZLN is a loosely libertarian socialist-aligned group which has run a large area of Chiapas in Mexico largely independently of government interference since 1994.

had close links with revolutionary syndicalism, radicals like Daniel De Leon, James Connolly and William Haywood, tend to be portrayed as a part of a broad anarchist tradition. In fact, these men were committed Marxists – state socialists. (Van der Walt and Schmidt 2009, Peacott 1991, *Anchorage Anarchy* 28 (2017) 1-9).

Contrary to Stirnerite egoists (discussed below) for anarchist communists the human individual is not sovereign, free to do whatever they like, using people and other life-forms purely as objects to be controlled and enjoyed. People have liberty only to the extent that they respect the integrity, well-being and equal liberty of other unique human beings. Liberty thus intrinsically entails equality and social solidarity – making up the three key values of radical Enlightenment and anarchist communism.

Second, anarchist communists completely reject the capitalist market economy, along with the wage system, private property, its competitive ethos, and the ideology of possessive individualism (egoism). In fact early class-struggle anarchists were fervently anti-capitalist, referring to the wage system as "wage slavery". Equally important, anarchist communists like Kropotkin agreed with Marx that there is a close and symbiotic relationship between state power and capitalism, whether this implied a laissez-faire system, welfare state, or state capitalism. Although of comparatively recent origin, throughout history the essential function of the state, for anarchist communists, has been to uphold systems of hierarchy and class exploitation, and the modern nation-state, with its representative government, is no different (Kropotkin 1993: 159-201).

The idea that it is only in recent years that capitalism has come to infiltrate the state, as suggested by such radical scholars as George Monbiot and Naomi Klein, is quite misconceived; state power and capitalism have always been linked, together with that of religion, forming what Ricardo Flores Magon[21] describes as the "dark trinity" (Morris 2018: 208, on Flores Magon see Bufe and Veryer 2005). Equally significantly, anarchist communists were emphasising, long before post-anarchists, that capitalism and the modern state were penetrating and "colonising" not only the natural world but all aspects of social life and culture.

Third, it expresses a vision of a society based solely on mutual aid and voluntary cooperation; a form of social organisation that would provide the fullest expression of human liberty and all forms of

---

21   The Flores Magon brothers Ricardo (1873-1922) and Enrique (1877-1954) were prominent indigenous figures whose work was influential as a precursor and ideological driver of the Mexican Revolution.

social life that exist independent of both the state and capitalism. Anarchist communists, as class struggle anarchists, thus believe in voluntary organisation, not in chaos, ephemerality, or "anything goes" and they view both tribal and kin-based societies and everyday social life in more complex societies as exhibiting some of the basic principles of anarchy. Both Reclus (1903) and Kropotkin (1902) were deeply interested in the social life and culture of tribal societies or "people without government" (Barclay 1082, Morris 2004; 2014B: 217-232). Anarchist communism is not, therefore, simply based on a future utopian ideal of a libertarian society, but on a socio-historical understanding of human social life and culture, for "anarchy" (as a social form) has long existed among humans. Anarchist communists were also expressing an "anarchistic sensibility" (the "spirit of revolt") long before pretentious postmodern egoists, those devotees of so-called "ontological anarchy" (Hakim Bey 1991, Newman 2016). Long ago, of course, Malatesta described freedom (liberty) as a "method" (Turcato 2014: 143).

Fourth, the anarchist communists grounded their political philosophy in a metaphysics that can be described as evolutionary naturalism (or emergent materialism). They were therefore ontological realists (like everyone else in their everyday social life), affirming that the material

17

world (nature) exists independently of human thought and symbolic culture. Realism, of course, is experienced every time a volcano erupts or we get lost in the woods, and is confirmed by the fact that the material world – according to the contemporary science – existed long before humans appeared.

As evolutionary (dialectical) naturalists, anarchist communists like Bakunin and Kropotkin held that the world (reality) consists exclusively of concrete material things, along with their dispositions, qualities, actions (events) and relations with other things. Life, consciousness and human symbolic culture, are, therefore, all emergent properties of material things, and have no independent existence. As such all things, including humans are unique, historical entities, with an enduring identity.

Anarchist communists, like Marxists, also embrace the radical aspects of the eighteenth century Enlightenment, namely: its stress on empirical reason – not the disembodied rationalism of Cartesian metaphysics which "philosophers" like Diderot had brought down to earth; empirical science, with its relational theory of knowledge; a rejection of knowledge based on authority, mystical intuition or divine revelation; an affirmation of universal human values such as liberty, solidarity and equality; and, finally, an ethical naturalism that based morality on our knowledge of human earthly life, not on subjective whims, Kantian duty, utility, the local culture or divine edicts.

In embracing these radical aspects of the Enlightenment the anarchist communists essentially adopted the philosophical materialism of Alexander von Humboldt, Charles Darwin,z Marx and other left-Hegelians. They thus tended to be critical of religion and all idealistic philosophy, whether subjective (Kant) absolutist (Hegel) or cultural (later to be adopted with enthusiasm by postmodernists.)[22]

---

22   **Morris note**: For a succinct discussion on the basic tenets and ideas of anarchist communism, as outlined by Errico Malatesta see Turcato (2014: 281).

Radical Alternatives
to Anarchist Communism

As anarchist communism developed as a political tradition in the years after the Paris Commune of 1871, it came to critique and to define itself in reference to four alternative radical traditions. These are Stirnerist egoism; individualist anarchism (or mutualism); authoritarian socialism (or Marxism); and religious anarchism. I will discuss each of these alternative radical tendencies in turn, and in the following section look at two anarchist currents that have emerged in recent decades. These are anarcho-primitivism and post-anarchism, which is largely a revamping of Stirner's egoism. All six radical traditions are living traditions. They have their contemporary adherents and have had a presence in the protests and demonstrations against global capitalism that have marked this century.

Stirner's Egoism

A Left-Hegelian and school teacher, Max Stirner – the pseudonym of Johann Schmidt – published in 1845 a book with the title *DER EINZIGE UND SEIN EIGENTUM*, usually translated as *The Ego and his*

Own (some prefer the translation *The Unique and its Property*). The book offers an important and radical critique of the state and all forms of religion. It also includes a critique of all concepts and "ideals" – whether justice, truth, freedom, equality, morality, love, humanity, reason and society – that, according to Stirner, have been given the status of a "sacred thing" (1913: 204) – or "spook" – thereby curtailing the liberty of the "unique one" – the individual human being. It's unclear how having an "ideal" – e.g. a concern for others – somehow inhibits a person's subjective agency.

The book has had a deep influence on anarchism, especially individualist anarchism, and Max Stirner has long been viewed as a key figure in the anarchist "pantheon". He is discussed in almost all histories of anarchism, and extracts from *The Ego and His Own* invariably find a place in Anarchist anthologies. But Stirner has generally been ignored by western philosophy, and, rather like Bookchin, his ideas have been ridiculed, denigrated, and misrepresented. He has even been described as a "mystic" and as a "solipsist", leading one of his devotees to suggest that Stirner is now regarded as something of a "bogeyman" (McQuinn 2000, for earlier studies of Stirner's philosophy see Carroll 1974, Clark 1976).

In many ways Stirner's politics represent liberal ideology taken to its extremes, in its strident proclamation of the ego – the unique individual human being – as a sovereign power, at liberty to do anything it wishes in the name of "self-affirmation" and "self-enjoyment" – at least if the "unique one" in its "oneness" has the power to do so.

Stirner has been described as "anti-philosophy", but in fact, he has his own brand of metaphysics embracing radical empiricism (phenomenalism), an extreme form of nominalism, and an atomistic epistemology[23]. This means that he continually confuses things and concepts – what he terms "spooks" for example. He variously describes the state, society and humanity as "spooks," as being merely ideas (or names) and having no reality. He tells us they are "nothings" as, for Stirner, only the "unique one" – the individual human being, the "corporeal self" as a "living, flesh-and-blood person" – is real (1973: 13). But of course, the state, and all forms of society, whatever their scale, are both real and unique, along with their artefacts and relations. Humanity, likewise, as a species being, is not a "spook" or simply a name, but refers to a population of real material things – human beings. Are elephants also "ghosts"?!

Stirner also makes a false dichotomy between the human subject as a human being and the human

---

23   Theory of knowledge

subject as a unique being, for the "unique one" is a human being, a biological organism, who not only has causal powers, dispositions and attributes that are not unique but common to all humans, but also, as a species being, is wholly dependent upon nature and other lifeforms for its very existence. Likewise, setting up a radical dichotomy between the individual ego – the unique one – and society which Stirner tends to view as a "spook" (a concept or name only) – is equally misleading, for humans are fundamentally social beings. Stirner's "atomistic" conception of the "unique one" is quite facile and limited (Clark 1976: 21).

In the introductory chapter to *The Ego and His Own* which is given the revealing title "All things are nothing to me", Stirner writes that as god and the sultan have been described as "egoists", why should he not be an "egoist" himself (1973: 4), that is, a sovereign power. No wonder one of his devotees should declare that "L'etat c'est moi" (the state that is me) (Hakim Bey 1991: 67) – which seems to be consonant with Stirner's own views. It is equally hardly surprising that Bookchin should write: "I can think of at least two people who did express these sweeping prerogatives: Joseph Stalin and Adolf Hitler" (1995B: 22).

Such egoism is surely not an anarchist sentiment, and hardly conducive to mutual aid and voluntary cooperation.

But perhaps Stirner's politics are best expressed in his own words:

> "Let us therefore not aspire to community ... but let us seek in others only means and organs which we may use as our property ... no one is my equal, but I regard him, equally with all other beings, as my property" (1973: 311).

> "My intercourse with the world, what does it aim at? I want to have the enjoyment of it, therefore it must be my property, and therefore I want to win it. I do not want the liberty of men, nor their equality, I want only my power over them. I want to make them my property, material for my enjoyment" (1973: 318).

Stirner concludes *The Ego and His Own* in nihilistic fashion with the words:

> "All things are nothing to me" (1973: 336).

For Stirner not only other people but also the natural world and all other forms have no intrinsic value; they are simply things to be controlled and employed as a "utility" or "property" to further the "unique one's" self-expression and self-enjoyment.

He seems to be completely devoid of any ecological sensibility and makes a fetish of self-interest and power over things and people. It is hardly surprising that the social anarchist John Clark should describe Stirner's thought as akin to the underlying assumptions of capitalism (1976: 57) as well as emphasising that Stirner had very little understanding of such values as community, social solidarity and mutual aid because he mainly had such an abstract conception of the human subject (1976: 97).

The left Hegelian Moses Hess long ago wrote that Stirner's ideal is a "bourgeois society, which takes the state to itself" (Stirner 2012: 95). This Stirner denied, suggesting that he was not opposed to socialism. Indeed the anarchist historian Max Nettlau[24] describes Stirner's thinking as, in substance, "eminently socialist" (1996: 54). Stirner, however, seems to advocate a rather narrow "union of egoists" and a politics of "insurrection" rather than social revolution involving a radical social transformation of existing institutions. (1973: 316). As Stirner put it, he was not interested in undermining the existing society, (capitalism and the state) but only in the

---

24   Nettlau (1865-1944) was perhaps the most important archivist of anarchist writings of his era. His extensive records were the foundation of the Institute of Social History in Amsterdam, which was almost named in his honour.

ego (himself) and its "ownness" (Bookchin 1995B: 54, Van der Walt and Schmidt 2009: 67).

Anarchist communists have rather mixed feelings about Stirner. On the one hand they applaud Stirner for his "revolt" against the state and all forms of authoritarian communism, and for extolling the free and full development of each person's "individuality". On the other hand, they find Stirner's "pure" individualism problematic, for it lacks any sense of responsibility towards other humans or towards the wider world. Kropotkin, for example, found Stirner's metaphysics too far removed from everyday social life and workers' struggles, and considered his amoral egoism as bordering on nihilism (Baldwin 1970 1 162)[25]. I discuss Stirner's egoism again in the next section, in relation to post-anarchism.

Individualist Anarchism

Individualist anarchism is a current of anarchist thought otherwise known as mutualism, or reformist anarchism. It takes its inspiration and key ideas from the French socialist Pierre-Joseph Proudhon, the American individualists Josiah Warren and Benjamin Tucker, and Stirner's egoism.

---

25 **Morris note**: For a useful discussion of Stirner's life and his relation to other Left Hegelians and anarchism see Shone (2014: 207-235)

Essentially, individualist anarchists seek to maintain the existing market economy shorn of its monopolies – in banking (money), tariffs, land and knowledge (the law of copyright). In many ways individualists aim to promote a form of anarchism that steers between two extremes: the rampant neoliberal capitalism espoused by the likes of Ayn Rand (1967), and the state socialism that is associated with the Marxists. Indeed Tucker writes of two distinct currents of socialist thought, namely state socialism and anarchism, identifying the latter with Proudhon's mutualism and individualist anarchism. Significantly, this current of thought rejects the state – defining an anarchist as anyone "who denies the necessity and legitimacy of government" (Tucker 1972: 3-16).

In terms of metaphysics individualist anarchists have a lot in common with libertarian socialists. For they advocate philosophical naturalism and a realist ontology[26]; warmly embrace Bakunin's atheism thereby repudiating all religious ontologies; adopt a ratio-empiricist[27] epistemology with its emphasis on human reason and human agency; and finally, acknowledge a form of ethical naturalism that seeks to "distil" from our understanding of nature, the contents

---

26   How a concept or thing is classified and explained.
27   The belief that all knowledge is derived from direct experience.

of a valid morality (Adan 1992: 33-48, 100). Of interest is that while Stirnerite egoists describe themselves as "anti-philosophy" (McQuinn 2000) individualist anarchists tend to depict themselves as philosophical anarchists"!

Yet it is significant that the individualist anarchists not only reject the authoritarian (state) socialism of the Marxists, but also – with equal fervour – the libertarian socialism of Bakunin and Kropotkin. The latter is dismissed as "collectivism" and this term is invariably employed in a derogatory sense. For in economic terms the individualist anarchists repudiate the idea of communism – the notion that the ownership and self-management of the; land and vital natural resources is undertaken by a local community. Indeed the very idea of the "commons" seems anathema to mutualists. With regard to the current issue of "the common versus commodities" (Ricoveri 2013) individualist anarchists side with the latter because, like all capitalists, the mutualists uphold the sanctity of "private property" in land and other resources. And property rights, as the 18th century legalist William Blackstone famously defined them, entail:

> "... the sole despotic dominion which one man claims and exercises over the external things of the world ... to the complete exclusion of other people's rights" (Bollier 2014: 98).

In terms of their politics the individualist anarchists advocate gradual change, and tend to reject any form of collective political action, opposing the very idea of "class struggle". Like Proudhon they therefore reject "strikes" by working people, viewing them as a form of violence. They strongly affirm liberty "both as ends and means" (Tucker 1972: 16, Van der Walt and Schmidt 2009: 84).

Always denying that they are in any way "anti-social" or "greedy capitalists", individualist anarchists place a strong emphasis on liberty. They therefore advocate free thought, free love, free press, free trade, free money, free competition and the free market. For what is characteristic of the mutualists is that they retain all the main trappings of a capitalist economy, shorn of the monopolies they associate with state power. They thus envisage a stateless society with the following: a market economy that highlights the virtue of competition in all spheres of life – "everywhere" as Tucker put it (1972: 15); a people's bank providing credit to anyone wishing to start their own business or cooperative enterprise; private property in land and basic resources, although emphasising that this involves only non-destructive rights; wage labour, while at the same time stressing that every person has a right to the products of their own labour; and finally,

an emphasis on the unique one as a rational ego –
who is virtually equated with Homo-economicus.
(Tucker 1972, Adam 1992, Peacott 1991: 5-7).

This strong emphasis on the liberty of the
individual ego means that individualist anarchists
tend to oppose "identity politics", specifically the
promotion of a particular social group or category
– race, ethnicity, nationality, gender, sexuality,
class etc – through the agencies of the state (Peacott
1991: 7).

Individualist anarchists, as indicated, tend to be
critical of anarchist communists, often depicting
them as crypto-authoritarians or even crypto-
Marxists. They accuse anarchist communists
of portraying ordinary people simply as passive
"victims" of oppressive systems, and thus come
to view themselves as an enlightened vanguard
elite, leading the struggles for a better world. This
is quite misleading, for anarchist communists
have always stressed that people should "act
for themselves" (Kropotkin 1988), and have always
sought to support or to engage in struggles
against the state and capitalism, without
attempting to dominate them, which would be
contrary to anarchist principles. Likewise, the
idea, constantly invoked by the mutualists, that
anarchist communists view society as somehow
prior to the individual, and that they wish to impose
communism upon everyone is equally misleading.

As Errico Malatesta long ago insisted, anarchist communists view communism as something that is freely accepted and is the "best guarantee for individual freedom". The idea of the "tyranny of the collectivity", for Malatesta, involves a complete misunderstanding of anarchist communism. Indeed, given that the latter entails a "libertarian" – individualist – outlook, there is no great divide, Malatesta felt, between the individualist anarchism and anarchist communism (V. Richards 1015: 23).

Unlike radical liberal ideology (which individualist anarchists seem to endorse), anarchist communists like Bakunin, Kropotkin, and Malatesta, neither conflate society with the state, nor view the relationship between individual human and social life as being one of opposition; rather for social anarchists, the relationship between the individual – "the unique one" – and society is always one that is dialectical, reciprocal and symbiotic. The idea that the human person is an "enemy" (no less) of society (Parker et al 2011) strikes all anarchist communists as completely facile. What Kropotkin and other anarchist communists advocate is "communal individualism" (Baldwin 1970: 123, Morris 2004: 74, Vodovnik 2013: 133).

Although anarchist communists always acknowledged that Proudhon, along with individualist anarchists like Lysander Spooner and Tucker, always expressed libertarian sentiments, and advocated a society without a state, they always expressed strong reservations about this form of anarchism.

Kropotkin, for example, objected strongly to its stress on egoism and the right of the individual to suppress other people if they have the power to do so; its affirmation of private property, petty-commodity production and the wage system (that is, a competitive market economy), and in justifying the use of violence to enforce agreements and to defend private property. All these positions were rejected by Kropotkin (Baldwin 1970: 172-73).

In recent decades there has also emerged a form of "libertarian anarchy", otherwise known as "anarcho-capitalism", which is specifically associated with the writings of Rothbard (Casey 2012). In its strident advocacy of free market capitalism, and in allowing private security firms, instead of the state, to protect private property and to control labour, libertarian anarchy can in no sense be described as anarchism. It is also doubtful whether Proudhon or the early individualist anarchists like Tucker, given their keen sense of liberty, would have approved of anarcho-capitalism. Indeed, contemporary individualist anarchists continue to affirm that they reject both capitalism and communism (Peacott 1991: 5).

Marxism

As I have discussed earlier, anarchist communism emerged as a political tradition during the 1870s, in opposition to Karl Marx and the state socialists that supported him within the First International. Thus from its inception anarchist communism has been highly critical of the kind of statist politics associated with Marx, and which later became known as social democracy, or simply Marxism. It is perhaps worth reflecting a little on Marx's own conception of socialism and the radical politics that he envisaged.

In the famous *Communist Manifesto* of 1848 Marx and Engels emphasised that the aim of the communist party would be the formation of the proletariat – the industrial working class – into a cohesive class and the "conquest of political power" by this class.

This would involve, they suggest, the need to "centralise all instruments of production in the hands of the state, centralisation of credit in the hands of the state by means of a national bank ... extension of factories and instruments of production owned by the state (and the) establishment of industrial armies, especially for agriculture" (Marx and Engels 1968: 52-53).

With its emphasis on the state controlling not only production but all spheres of social life, Marx's vision is the complete antithesis to that of Proudhon – who advocated a market society based on petty-commodity production.

Two years later, in their address to the Communist League, Marx and Engels again stressed that it should strive not only for "the one and invisible German republic" but also the most "decisive centralisation" of power in the hands of the state. The revolutionary party in Germany, they suggest, must aim at state control, and under no circumstances could the local autonomy of any village, town or province be tolerated (Marx 1973: 328-29).

It is hardly surprising then, that within the International Working Men's association, which as G. D. H. Cole suggests was largely a "trade union affair" (1954: 38), Marx should endeavour to create a centralised political party that sought the "conquest of political power", thereby establishing the dictatorship of the proletariat" – a "workers' state".

Bakunin and the anarchist communists, of course, always stressed that the parliamentary road to socialism would only lead to reformism while the "seizure of state power" by the communist party on behalf of the working class – as with the Bolsheviks and later the Maoists – would inevitably lead to tyranny and state capitalism. And history seems to have proved Bakunin and the anarchist communists right on both counts.

There has, of course, been an absolute welter of books and articles discussing and debating the relationship between Marxism and anarchism[28]. But anarchist communists have always stood firm in rejecting the statist politics of the Marxists, whether of the parliamentary variety – as expressed by, for example, the Socialist Party of Great Britain – or the more tyrannical version of Lenin and Mao, which, essentially, is a form of state capitalism under a party dictatorship.

Religious anarchism

Until comparatively recently religious anarchism has mainly been associated with the life and learnings of three religious visionaries, namely, Leo Tolstoy, Nicolas Berdyaev and Mohandas Gandhi. All three have been described as anarchists.

---

28 **Morris note**: A recent collection entitled *Libertarian Socialism* (Pritchard et al 2017) aims to bring together Marxism (red, socialism) and anarchism (black, libertarian). Significantly, the book makes no mention of Bakunin, Goldman, Malatesta, Landauer and Rocker who were long ago advocating real libertarian socialism, while offering ample discussion of Lenin, Trotsky and Gramsci, as well as Marx himself, who were certainly not libertarians. There seems to be an attempt to re-brand Marxism as a form of libertarian socialism, but see review by McKay (2014).

Around 1879 Tolstoy, a world-famous literary figure as the author of *War and Peace*, had a mid-life crisis. He was then aged 50. For after a close reading of the Christian gospels, Tolstoy became convinced that violence was contrary to the human spirit and human freedom. He thus rejected his earlier lifestyle as a member of the Russian aristocracy, and came to oppose all forms of what Tolstoy described as "slavery". He therefore expressed his strong opposition to the state (along with militarism and patriotism), the capitalist market economy (along with private property, money, wage-labour and share-cropping) and the practises of the Russian Orthodox Church – indeed all forms of coercive authority.

In 1886, this "crackpot" (as Lenin described Tolstoy) published a seminal book entitled *What Then Must we Do*, outlining his political credo (see my review 1996: 158-160). Tolstoy's religious philosophy affirmed the importance of reason, love and creative work as essential to human well-being, and although he never described himself as an anarchist (associating anarchism with revolutionary violence) he was opposed to liberal reformism, and can be described as an advocate of nonviolent revolution. He was therefore a nonviolent religious anarchist (David Stephens in Tolstoy 1990: 7-19).

Tolstoy seems to have been influenced mainly by Proudhon, who he met in Paris in 1861, and the American socialist, Henry George. But Tolstoy rejected George's land nationalisation scheme – expressed in his widely-acclaimed book *Progress and Poverty* (1879) – as it presupposed the jurisdiction of a bureaucratic state. This Tolstoy vehemently opposed, concluding that "slavery" in our time is "produced in the violence of militarism, by the appropriation of the land, and by the exaction of money" (Tolstoy 1991: 109).[29]

Although a religious mystic like Tolstoy, Nicolas Berdyaev was in many ways very different from the novelist, as he remained closely attached to Russian Orthodox Christianity, and rejected Tolstoy's pacifism. Berdyaev spent much of his life in Paris, and in the late 1940s was widely acclaimed as an important religious philosopher. He is now virtually forgotten. Given his emphasis on human freedom – even our relationship with the material world is, according to Berdyaev, a form of "bondage" – it is hardly surprising that he is considered an anarchist, along with Dorothy Day and Simone Weil. He is described as an advocate of **Christianarchy** (Marshall 1992: 84, John 1995).

But Berdyaev was not an anarchist. He repudiated anarchism, and in *Slavery and Freedom* he wrote that the idea of a stateless society – where

---

29   **Morris note**: On Tolstoy's anarchism see Woodcock 1962: 207-219, Hopton 2010.

communal individuality thrives – is a "lie and seductive illusion" and that the state is necessary to guarantee human freedom. The role of the state, Berdyaev writes, "consists in the protection and preservation" of human rights (1943: 147-49). This is hardly an anarchist sentiment.

Gandhi, of course, has long been recognised as an inspiration for many communitarian anarchists, who advocate a nonviolent form of social revolution, as well as inspiring such iconic figures as Martin Luther King and Vandana Shiva. His legacy was particularly important in the forming of the Sarvodaya "welfare of all" movement in Sri Lanka by the Buddhist teacher Dr. A. T Ariyaratne, which aimed to establish a "commonwealth of villages" (Clark 2013: 217-45).

But it has always puzzled anarchists as to why Gandhi, who described himself as a kind of anarchist, and who admired the ideals of Tolstoy and Kropotkin, who was profoundly anti-militarist, and who wanted to create a decentralised, libertarian agrarian society, came to be used simply as a tool of the Indian national bourgeoisie. Certainly Gandhi came from a wealthy middle-class background, and it is equally salient that all his activities (whether in respect to his ashram or the Congress party) were financially supported by business interests, vast sums of money being given by wealthy industrialists such as G. D. Birla. It is important to note, too, that Gandhi always shied away from supporting any direct challenges to the status quo, and declined to support the untouchables in their efforts to enter Brahmin temples and the rural peasants in their rent strikes. As many scholars have noted, Gandhi always sought to maintain harmony between peasants and landlords, and between capital and labour. But the striking discrepancy between Gandhi's political vision and anarchy, and his actual political practises is certainly noteworthy (Morris 1996: 67-71).

But both Gandhi's philosophy and his actual politics are very different from that of the anarchist communists. For Gandhi was a religious mystic and although somewhat eclectic in his religious beliefs, declaring that God was both "truth" and "love" he essentially remained within the Hindu fold, particularly that of Advaita Vedanta[30] (Richards 1982: 2-3). In his practical politics outside of his ashram Gandhi can hardly be described as an anarchist for he was an ardent Indian nationalist, and throughout the 1940s whole-heartedly supported the foundation of India as an independent secular nation-state.

During the last few decades numerous scholars have been eager to promote (having abandoned

---

30   A spiritual practice aimed at disentangling the true self from the body and mind.

moribund Christianity) some esoteric religious metaphysic by linking it with anarchism, allegedly to "revitalise" the "revolutionary movement" at a time of ecological crisis. Thus Sebastian Job presents us with the "entheogenic challenge", advocating taking drugs, specifically toad venom and ayahuasca, in order to experience the "divine within". In the process Job disparages Bakunin's atheism as being "modern", and arrogantly suggests that he and Bookchin are somehow "lost" in the modern world. (Job 2016: 88).

Other scholars have been equally eager to provide some form of esoteric religious mysticism as a metaphysic, whether in the form of theosophy, transcendentalism, Islamic mysticism or New Age spirituality. We are thus urged to resist the modern secular state by offering our "submission" (no less) to some higher power or authority, that of the universal spirit or divinity, otherwise known as god (or Allah) (Hakim Bey 1991, Cudenec 2013: 73-88, Vodovnik 2013: 159).

Three points may be made in the present context.

First, esoteric religions, mysticism rather than "revitalising" anarchism simply offer an atavistic spiritualist metaphysic, turning anarchism into some kind of esoteric spirit cult. But as Bookchin warned, to worship or reverie any being, natural or supernatural – specifically that of a world spirit (anima mundi) – "will always be a form of self-subjugation and servitude that ultimately yields social domination ... the moment human beings fall to their knees before any thing that is "higher" than themselves hierarchy will have made its first triumph over freedom" (Bookchin 1989:13). As Kropotkin recognised, the first forms of hierarchy began with the shamanic rituals of tribal peoples – now being extolled by Sebastian Job (Morris 2004: 180 cf Zerzan 1994)!

Second, atheism has never been "modern", for evolutionary naturalism (emergent materialism and atheism) has never been a part of "capitalist modernity", Indeed, as a philosophical tradition, it has always been marginalised, ridiculed, ignored and disparaged by those in power. It is noteworthy that the iconic figures of western philosophy, for example, Descartes, Leibniz, Kant, Hegel, Schelling, Husserl, Bergson, Heidegger, Whitehead and Wittgenstein have all been religious thinkers – philosophical idealists – as well as pro-state (though Wittgenstein did express his admiration for Tolstoy). Equally important, as Bakunin and anarchist communists have long emphasised, throughout human history there has been a close and symbiotic relationship between political power and religious mysticism At the present time the "modern" states of Turkey, India, Saudi Arabia and China, as well as the United States of America, all happily combine autocratic state politics with an ardent embrace of global capitalism and state advocacy of the kind of esoteric religious mysticism that some anarchists now wish to promote as an alternative to evolutionary naturalism. The state, capitalism and esoteric religion have long formed the "sacred bundle" of "modernity", or what Flores Magon described as the "dark trinity". Esoteric mysticism began as the "religion of empires" (Morris 2018: 209-211).

Third, throughout human history and in a wide range of human societies, people have employed an enormous variety of material substances, but especially fungi and psychotropic plants to induce trance states or visionary experiences, specifically to communicate with a wide variety of spiritual beings. These may include the holy spirit, angels, spirits of the dead, native spirits and a host of spiritual beings specific to a particular culture, such as, for example, the Nature spirits (Berma), Voodoo spirits (Haiti) and the Zar spirits (Sudan).

But drugs are not necessary to induce either a gnostic experience or an ecstatic or shamanic state of consciousness. This can be done quite easily through meditative states, rhythmic chanting and drumming, or any intense physical movement, sensual and social deprivation (isolation, fasting, exposure to extreme temperatures), and physical pain (including torture). In fact, any material substance or activity that puts the human body under acute stress may induce an altered state of consciousness. How such changes of state are interpreted – whether for example drinking wine to excess leads to simple inebriation or possession by the god Dionysius – depends on a person's beliefs and on a specific cultural context.[31]

But whether engaging in such spirit rituals, or seeking some esoteric mystical experience – both of which imply the acceptance of a religious (spiritualist) ontology whether expressed as polytheism, theism or panentheism – can play any role in "revitalising" anarchism as a political tradition is debatable to say the least. At a time of acute ecological crisis, evolutionary naturalism, it seems to me, is a more reliable guide to action, than adopting some esoteric other-worldly religious metaphysics.

Anarchist communists have never been opposed to religion as a personal worldview, acknowledging that people should have the freedom, as Joe Peacott put it, "to believe anything one wishes no matter how foolish, whether god/dess, gaia or the cosmic muffins" (1991: 9). Anarchist communists have also long recognised that the meaning and the social and political impact of a religion can only be

---

31   On the anthropology of religion see Morris 2006

understood if situated within its socio-historical context (Morris 2006). Thus in specific contexts religious movements, such as the Brethren of the Free Spirits and the "Diggers" associated with Gerard Winstanley, may express an anarchistic sensibility and an ethic of communalism (Rexruth 1975).

But during the past two millennia, as anarchist communists have long emphasised – and as indicated above – religious beliefs and practises have historically been intrinsically connected with state power, serving to sanctify and uphold systems of political domination, even of the most tyrannical states.

Anarcho-Primitivism
and Post-Anarchism

In the closing decades of the twentieth century academic scholars began informing us that we had come to "the end of history", that the nation-state was in terminal decline, and that liberal capitalism had emerged "triumphant" over all its adversaries. There was, then, "no alternative" to global capitalism, or at least none that could be envisaged. All that we could do, the guru of New Labour told us, was argue about "how far and in what ways capitalism should be governed or regulated" (Giddens 1998:43, see my critique of Giddens' politics of the "third way" Morris 1996: 178-182).

The new era of global capitalism – postmodernity – also saw the emergence and flourishing of a new philosophical ethos, widely described as postmodernism. It became all the rage in philosophy, anthropology and the social sciences more generally. It was accompanied by a plethora of other "post" scenarios – post-structuralism, post-feminism, post-Marxism and post-humanism. There were even post-animals around, but these are not to be confused with the real badgers and dormice that inhabit the woods and fields. Not surprisingly there emerged in the 1990s several "new" and "post" forms of anarchism.

Described as the "new anarchism" (Kinna 2005) they included the following libertarian currents: anarcho-capitalism, a re-affirmation of Stirner's egoism, the poetic terrorism (Nietzschean aesthetics) associated with Hakim Bey, anarcho-primitivism and so-called postmodern anarchism, otherwise known as post-structuralist anarchism, or simply post-anarchism (Rousselle and Evren 2011).

These distinct anarchist currents were interrelated – the journal *Anarchy*, for example, combining an advocacy of both anarcho-primitivism and Stirnerite egoism – but all declared that the anarchism of an earlier generation of anarchists – that is, the anarchist communism of Bakunin, Kropotkin, Goldman, Malatesta and Rocker – was now deemed "old" anarchism. It was viewed as old-fashioned, out-dated, politically redundant, an "historical baggage" that needed to be rejected, or at least given an overhaul (Purkis and Bowen 1997: 3).

In the pages of the *Green Anarchist*, anarcho-primitivist writer John Moore described Kropotkin's anarchist communism as now "obsolete". In the wake of the anti-globalisation demonstrations, at the turn of the present century, the autonomous Marxist John Holloway, in a highly popular text *Change the World Without Taking Power* also intimated that anarchism was no longer "relevant" to contemporary radical activists (2002: 21). In the process, of course, appropriating all the basic ideas of anarchist communism without any acknowledgement.

I have elsewhere offered some critical reflections on the so-called "new anarchism", suggesting that there is in fact very little that is novel or even original, in these diverse currents of libertarian politics. For many of these currents have been around since the end of the nineteenth century (Morris 2014B: 133-145). Here I shall focus on the two more prominent anarchist tendencies that re-emerged at the end of the last century – anarcho-primitivism and post-anarchism.

Anarcho-Primitivism

Primitivism as a political doctrine – the idyll of the golden age of hunter-gatherers – is as old as the hills (not quite!) for it goes back to antiquity, and to the beginnings of settled agriculture and the rise of the early states (see Lovejoy and Boas 1935). It is particularly associated with the Enlightenment philosopher Jean-Jacques Rousseau and the concept of the "noble savage". The key figures in linking ancient primitivism with contemporary anarchist politics; Fredy Perlman (1983) and John Zerzan (1994), view "civilization" – interpreted as "Leviathan" or the "Beast" – as the prime factor both in undermining human freedoms and in the emergence of the present environmental crisis.

John Zerzan presents us with an apocalyptic, even perhaps a gnostic vision. Our hunter-gatherer past is described as an idyllic era of virtue, freedom and authentic living. The last 8,000 years of human history, in contrast, after the rise of agriculture (with the domestication of plants and animals) – or the "fall" – is seen by contrast as a period of tyranny, exploitation and hierarchical control, a mechanised routine devoid of any joy or spontaneity. Human civilization is also viewed by Zerzan as involving a loss of contact by humans with the natural world and thus a continuing degradation of the environment. All those products of human civilizations and the creative human imagination – farming, art, philosophy, technology, science, writing, urban living, symbolic culture, are viewed by Zerzan negatively, and denigrated by the anarchist in the most monolithic fashion.

The future, we are told, is "primitive". How on earth (literally!) this can be achieved in a world of more than six billion people (for evidence suggests that the hunter-gatherer lifestyle is only able to support one or two people per square mile) or whether the "future primitive" actually entails a return to hunter-gatherer subsistence, Zerzan does not tell us.

Whether such images of "green primitivism" are symptomatic of the estrangement of affluent city-dwellers and intellectuals from the natural (and human) world, as Roy Ellen (1986) and Bookchin (1995A: 120-46) both suggest, I will leave for the reader to judge.

But what is important and seminal about Zerzan's work I think is the affirmation that hunter-gatherers are in many ways "stone-age anarchists". As Zerzan put it: life in "primitive" society was largely one of leisure, gender equality, intimacy with the natural world and a sensuous wisdom, based on organic relationships, not on language. The fact that hunter-gatherers, and tribal peoples generally, express an anarchist sensibility was, of course, long ago emphasised by Peter Kropotkin, as well as by Bookchin. Kropotkin, for example, noted the close intimacy that exists in tribal societies between humans and animals; that such people have an encyclopaedic knowledge of the natural world, and place a marked emphasis on sharing, generosity and mutual aid, as well as an equal emphasis on individual autonomy and independence (Kropotkin 1902: 74-101, Morris 2004: 173-190); Likewise Bookchin in his *The Ecology of Freedom* (1982) devotes a chapter to what he describes as "organic society" – early hunter-gatherers and tribal societies. Bookchin describes the world-view of such societies as having the following characteristics: a stress on equality and the absence of coercive or domineering values; a feeling of unity between the individual and the community; a sense of common property and an emphasis on mutual aid and (non-destructive) rights; and finally, an ecological sensibility involving a relationship with the natural world that is one of reciprocal harmony rather than of domination (Bookchin 1982: 43-61).

But both Kropotkin and Bookchin were only too aware of the limitations of a hunter-gatherer existence and tribal life, and were therefore concerned that we draw inspiration and lessons from the past, and from tribal societies more especially, rather than romanticising them. Still less that we should attempt to emulate them. Given the vital importance of symbolic culture, technology, city life, and the possibility of creating an "ecological civilization" and a truly democratic society, and given also the present human population on earth, for anarchist communists like Bookchin the "future primitive" of John Zerzan is simply not an option. (Morris 2014B: 141-42; for a useful discussion of anarchism versus primitivism see Sheppard 2003; for a sympathetic and illuminating account of Zerzan's critique of symbolic thought see Young 2013; on the anarchist solidarity of contemporary foragers see Morris 2014B: 217-37, 2018: 244-47).

Post-Anarchism

During the past 30 years, at the very time when global capitalism was being declared "triumphant", numerous protests and demonstrations were erupting throughout the world – whether against some autocratic regime, or against the incursions or inequalities of neoliberal capitalism. Resistance and opposition to global capitalism was especially well exemplified in the anti-globalisation movement that emerged in the wake of demonstrations against the World Trade organisation in Seattle in 1999, and in the Occupy movement that suddenly erupted in 2011 in many major cities (Graeber 2013, Morris 2014B: 102-08). Although such protest movements invariably reach the attention of both the media and academic scholarship, throughout the world tribal peoples and peasant communities are also actively defending their lands and their livelihood from the intrusions and onslaught of neoliberal capitalism. their protests, however, hardly ever reach the media. A specific example is the struggles of tribal peoples (Adivasi) in India against the large mining corporations, which are backed by the Indian state (Padel and Das 2010).

The protests and demonstrations associated with the anti-capitalist movement were not specifically anarchist, for the movement embraced people from right across the spectrum of radical politics – trade unionists defending their jobs, a plethora of NGOs concerned with issues of social justice, indigenous activists, radical liberal scholars like Susan George and Naomi Klein who resent the fact that society is being subordinated to the interests of the large corporations, feminists, Marxists, Earth First![32] and various other environmental groupings, as well as anarchists of diverse tendencies (Tormey 2004, Morris 2014B: 102-08). But as many scholars have indicated, at the "heart" of the anti-globalisation and Occupy[33] movements were anarchists; even more significant is that the "ethos" of these movements reflected the "libertarian spirit" of anarchist communism. (Vodovnik 2013). For this ethos involves the basic principles of anarchist communism denoted above: a rejection of statist politics, whether that of liberal democracy, or the vanguard party of the Marxists; the advocacy of new forms of direct or participatory democracy; a rejection of the possessive individualism (egoism) that is intrinsic to neoliberal capitalism; the

---

32   Earth First! Is a green direct-actionist group organised along anarchist lines. Established in the 1970s, it has been at the heart of many major confrontations with state-backed projects, notably in Britain the anti-roads protest movement of the 1990s.

33   Occupy was part of a wave of temporary camps which took over public spaces particularly in the US and Britain in 2011, mirroring the efforts of the Indignados in Spain and Greece, and the Tahrir Square occupation in Egypt.

affirmation of the need for a social revolution (going beyond the "spirit of revolt") reflected in the adage of the World Social Forum[34] "another world is possible" (Fisher and Ponniah 2003); an emphasis on "the freedom of equals"; and, finally, the need to create new social forms and institutions based on mutual aid and voluntary cooperation. This did not entail the advent of a "new form of politics", as some political theorists contend, but the resurgence and the reaffirmation of a form of politics – anarchist communism – that has been around, and has continually been erupting, since the end of the nineteenth century. Equating the anarchism expressed in the demonstrations and radical social movements of the present century with "post-anarchism" (Newman 2016) is not only misleading, but quite facile. At the "heart" of the anti-capitalist movement were old-fashioned narchist communists (libertarian socialists). (Sheehan 2003:12, Franks 2006:162). Indeed so-called post-anarchism which emerged in the 1990s is hardly novel: it is the latest expression of Stirnerite egoism which has been around for more than a century, alongside individualist anarchism (see Parker et al 2011).

---

34   The World Social Forum was set up in 2001 as a direct alternative to the World Economic Forum, and has gathered social resistance organisations from around the world to coordinate and share knowledge about the advance of neoliberal activity.

There is, then, nothing particularly new or original about post-anarchism, although its academic devotes may offer interesting reflections and insights on many contemporary political issues. For postmodernism is neither a "new paradigm" (in a philosophical sense) nor is it a "new form of politics", given that it is largely a revamping of Max Stirner's radical individualism (egoism).

Largely the invention of university academics, post-anarchism is particularly associated with the writings of Hakim Bey (1991) (aka Peter Lamborn Wilson), Todd May (1994), Lewis Call (2002), and Saul Newman (2001, 2016). It is essentially the outcome of a critical engagement or synthesis between postmodernism (and post-structuralism) and anarchist theory, as the latter is reflected in the writings of Proudhon, Bakunin, Kropotkin and Goldman. Indeed, post-anarchists, while filling pages of text with esoteric discussions of Michel Foucault, Jacques Lecan, Jean-Francois Lyotard, Ernesto Lacan and Alain Badiou – none of whom are anarchists, post-structuralist or otherwise – hardly ever mention any other anarchist. The tendency of post-anarchists to describe Bakunin and Kropotkin as "classical" anarchists, is equally problematic, given the diversity within the anarchist tradition. As Noam Chomsky emphasised, anarchism is a very broad category, embracing many different political tendencies (2005: 234).

Postmodernism, as earlier indicated, is a rather cultural movement or philosophical ethos that came into prominence in the closing decades of the twentieth century. It took its main inspiration from the writings of Hegel, Nietzsche, Heidegger and Wittgenstein – all political reactionaries – and it included scholars with radically different approaches to philosophy and social life. But as an intellectual ethos it is particularly associated with such scholars as Baudrillard, Lacan, Derrida, Foucault, Rorty, Laclau and Judith Butler (Sim 2005). It is characterised by the following three tenets:

Firstly, as (supposedly) we have no knowledge of the world except through "descriptions", to employ Richard Rorty's term (1989: 5) – the "real" is conceived as an effect on even the creation of discourses.

This notion is perhaps best illustrated by a quotation from one anthropologist who described his own theory as …

> "consistent with the position of the *idealist* wing of ethno-methodology that there is *no reality* independent of the words (texts, signs, documents and so on) used to apprehend it. In other words, reality is constituted in and through discourse" (Woolgar 1986: 312, my italics).

Thus throughout the latter part of the 20th century scholars, from a wide range of backgrounds, were telling us that nature (the material world world) – even tigers – were not real but some social constructions; that human beings – philosophers especially! – create the "worlds" in which they live; that there is no objective reality; or even, as the title of one book put it, "nature is culture" (Seeland 1997).

Postmodernism thus extols an anti-realist metaphysic. Indeed postmodernism (as embraced by post-anarchists) is virtually the apotheosis of the "correlationism" – the anti-realism – that has dominated Western philosophy throughout the twentieth century. Correlationism is the philosophical doctrine that there is no world without humans, and no humans without a world – hence the "correlation" – implying that there is no real world independent of human cognition and human culture. Such "correlationism", it is argued, by many recent scholars, characterises most of the last century, namely, Hegelian Marxism, neo-Kantian hermeneutics[35], phenomenology[36], existentialism, structuralism, post-structuralism – and, of course, postmodernism (Bryant et al 2011:3, Gratton 2014).

---

35   The theory and practice of interpretation.
36   A philosophical emphasis on the structures of experience, ie. consciousness, the imagination, interpersonal relationships etc.

Postmodernism, as adopted by the post-anarchists, is thus fundamentally an anti-realist metaphysic, and like Stirner, tends to conflate things with their concepts.

Secondly, in an extravagant reaction to Cartesian rationalism and Edmund Husserl's phenomenology, postmodernism proclaims the "dissolution" or the "end of man" (Foucault 1970: 387). The human subject thus tends to be portrayed as the "product" or the "effect" of either ideology, or power or language (discourses). As expressed, for example, by Foucault: "the individual (no less!) is the product of power" (in Deleuze and Guattari 1977: xiv) or by a literary critic: "it is through language that people constitute themselves as subjects" (Belsey 1980: 159). Although the "subject" is given various meanings by postmodernists, there is a general tendency to go to extremes, either viewing the subject as simply socially determined by language, power, or ideology, – and thus lacking agency – or reducing the subject to a unique, abstract individual – the ego – who is free to create "oneself" (May 1994: 131). But pervasive in postmodernism is the downplaying of the human (organic) aspects of human subjectivity. Not surprisingly, the ego (or self) is viewed as a "blank slate" or "void", leading postmodernists to declare in oracular fashion that there is no such thing as "human nature" (May 1994: 97, Koch 2011: 39).

Given the extensive knowledge we now have about human biology, derived from evolutionary biology, genetics and cognitive neuroscience, the suggestion that there is no human nature has been described by one scholar – a devotee of Bakunin – as simply "absurd" (McLaughlin 2002: 249). But one thing is clear: postmodernism)along with post-anarchism) is fundamentally anti-humanist, tending to completely oblate human biology, and to de-naturalise the human subject. It is debatable whether either Stirner or Nietzsche went to such an extreme as their postmodern disciples.[37]

Thirdly, in rejecting both Cartesian metaphysics and "meta – narratives" – supposedly the defining characteristic of postmodernism (Lyotard 1984) – postmodernists highlight the virtues of what is described as the "postmodern condition" – fragmentation, alienation, ephemerality, contingency, nihilism, cultural pastiche, relativism and egoism. But rather than being a new intellectual paradigm as some post-anarchists suppose, postmodernism is best described as the culture or even the "logic" of global capitalism (Jameson 1998: 20).

---

37   **Morris note**: Stirner as a nominalist was essentially a vulgar materialist, while recent scholarship has emphasised that Nietzsche not only stood firmly in the tradition of the Enlightenment, but was fundamentally a biological thinker and a philosophical naturalist. (Richardson 2004, on the varied interpretations of Nietzsche see Morris 2014A: 572-79).

All this has led the acolytes of postmodernism to proclaim, with some stridency, the "dissolution" or "erasure" or the "end" of such concepts as truth, reason, history, class, nature, the self (declared as illusion), and even philosophy – along with the Enlightenment itself. Yet in their rejection of history and class, in reducing social reality to discourses, in their epistemological and moral relativism, in their "dissolution" of the human subject", or alternatively its reduction to the ego, and, finally, in their seeming obsession with high-tech cyberspace, many scholars have remarked that there is an "unholy alliance" between postmodernism and the triumphalism of neoliberal capitalism (Wood and Foster 1997).

Postmodernism has, of course, been subjected to a barrage of criticisms by scholars from very diverse backgrounds; liberal philosophers, Marxists, anthropologists, cultural materialists, as well as anarchists – in particular the important critiques of **Zerzan and Bookchin** (Gellner 1992, Bunge 1996, Harris 1995, Detmer 2003, Zerzan 1994: 101-134, Bookchin 1995A: 172-204)[38]

Given these critiques, it would be difficult to find anyone these days, apart from post-anarchists, claiming to be a postmodernist.

---

38   **Morris note**: Some 20 years ago (1997), in an essay significantly entitled 'In Defence of Realism and Truth' I offered my own critical reflections of postmodernism, then at the zenith of its popularity, among the anthropological followers of Heidegger (Morris 2014B: 26-56).

Although post-structuralism has often been described as the philosophy of postmodernism, it is of interest that all the radical scholars that have most appeal to postmodernists – Foucault, Derrida, Deleuze and Guattari (May 1994, Newman 2001) – expressed an opposition to postmodernism, or at least distanced themselves from it. The term "post-structuralism" is, of course, completely vacuous, given the extreme diversity – both in philosophy and politics – among scholars who have been labelled post-structuralists. Post-anarchists like Newman seem to cherry pick the ideas of a wide range of political theorists – for example Slavoj Zizek, Jacques Ranciere, Reiner Schurmann, Jean-Luc Nancy, Alain Badiou, Lacan and Giorgio Agamben – whoever is the flavour of the year – in order to critique and thus undermine anarchist communism and its politics – of revolutionary class struggle anarchism.

Let me now then turn to the so-called "post-structuralist" critique of social anarchism, specifically anarchist communism.

The Post-Structuralist Critique of Anarchist Communism

It has to be recognised that very few of the libertarian ideas expressed by post-structuralist philosophers – such as their critiques of sovereignty and statist politics – are in fact new or original. For what they have done is simply appropriate the basic ideas and principles of anarchist communism (social anarchism), and wrap them up in scholastic jargon with little or no acknowledgement of the early anarchists. For example, Gilles Deleuze can write, in discussing French capitalism that:

> "Against this global policy of power, we must initiate localised counter-responses, skirmishes, active and occasionally preventive defences. We have no need to totalise that which is invariably totalised on the side of power; if we were to move in this direction, it would mean restoring the representative forms of centralism and a hierarchical structure" (quoted in Foucault 1977: 212).

Deleuze seems singularly unaware that this anti-state strategy had been advocated by anarchist communists for more than a hundred years.

In discussing the post-structuralist critique of anarchism, or rather the post-anarchist critique of anarchist communism (Newman 2016), I shall focus on three topics, namely, power, the human subject and social revolution. But three other points may be made in the present context.

First; although post (structuralist) anarchist theory (May 1994, Newman 2001) focuses mainly on a select number of post-structuralists – Lacan, Foucault, Lyotard, Derrida, and Deleuze – it is worth noting that none of these scholars ever provided any critique of social anarchism. Indeed, as members of a "privileged French mandarin caste" – as Marshall Berman describes them – none of these post-structuralists evinced any real interest in anarchist communism, either as a historical movement or a political tradition.

Second, the "post-anarchists" do not really offer a critique of anarchist communism; they rather tend to misrepresent the ideas and political vision of early anarchists like Bakunin and Kropotkin. For in order to erect a radical dichotomy between anarchist communism and a self-identified post-structuralism or "post-anarchism" (May 1994, Newman 2001), they indicate poor scholarly engagement with the writings of the early anarchists, and thus present an inaccurate interpretation of their radical politics (Jun 2011: 236).

Finally, while Lewis Call (2002) advocates a "postmodern" version of anarchism, and Saul Newman (2016) a form of postmodern egoism as a radically new "post-anarchism" (actually, as indicated above, a revamping of Stirner's egoism), Todd May in contrast has recently explicitly denied that he is a "post-anarchist". Distancing himself from the philosophical ethos of postmodernism, and making no mention of Stirner in his early study (1994), May affirms that there is nothing "post" about the post-structuralist anarchism of Foucault, Deleuze, Derrida and Lyotard, and that their politics are but a "continuation" (with added insights) of earlier anarchist (communist) tradition (2018: 339).

Apart from Deleuze at odd moments, whether any of these post-structuralist philosophers can be considered anarchists is debatable. Foucault, for example, though often described as a "neo-anarchist", dismissed anarchism as "infantile" and supported the Ayatollah Khomeini and the Islamic clerics at the time of the Iranian revolution. He was also happy to serve as a functionary for the French state. Likewise Lyotard seems to have ended his days dreaming of intergalactic travel and supporting right-winger Giscard D'Estaing in the French presidential elections. Few of the other scholars who have been described as "post-structuralists" – for example Bourdieu, Rorty and Baudrillard – are in any sense anarchists (Morris 2018: 197-99).

Power

The so-called post-structuralist critique expressed by a variety of scholars (but especially May 1994.Newman 2001, Morland 2004) suggests that early anarchists were simply and narrowly anti-state, that they viewed power only as repressive and coercive, and that they were unaware of other forms of power, or that power could be "productive". As I have discussed elsewhere (Morris 2014 B; 175-78), these criticisms are quite misleading and misrepresent the politics of early anarchist communists.

For over a hundred years social scientists, political theorists and anarchist communists, have all recognised that no hegemonic power or political ruler, not even the most bloodthirsty tyrant, rules solely by means of repression and coercion. They thus seek the wider "voluntary servitude" on the part of the oppressed and exploited – an old[39] conception that has become something of a fetish among post-anarchists (see Newman 2016: 91-112).

---

39   **Morris note**: It seems odd that in a book specifically on contemporary anarchism, and with a whole chapter focused on "voluntary servitude", that Newman should make no mention at all of Chomsky's critique of the modern media and what he describes as the "manufacture of consent" (Peck 1989: 121-36, Herman and Chomsky 1988).

It is noteworthy that over 40 years ago class struggle anarchists were expressing the view that:

> "Since in the long run rule must be by consent, there is in addition to rule by the whip (coercive power) an apparatus of rule by persuasion, by brainwashing and mental conditioning and the whole process of education" (Christie and Meltzer 2010: 15).

Anarchist communists have therefore long recognised that power – that is state power, in its various institutional forms, produces prisons, educational institutions like schools, forms of knowledge that often serve as state propaganda, festivals, disciplined subjects, and ideologies – specifically nationalism and religion. Long before Foucault, anarchist communists opposed all these "technologies" of power, and recognised that religion is an early form of power.

But whereas Foucault and Deleuze as Nietzschean Marxists called for the "reform" of prisons, Kropotkin advocated a complete abolition of the prison system (see Davis 2003). Kropotkin and the anarchist communists did not view the state as the "root of all evil" (Brown 1993: 157) but opposed all forms of power – especially capitalist exploitation, all state ideologies, and indeed all forms of power that inhibited the free and full development of the unique human individual (Bakunin in Lehning 1973: 196).

It was obvious to anarchist communists that state power "produced" subjects – prisoners, slaves and wage labourers. But they also recognised that such power did not produce the unique living individuals who were imprisoned and enslaved – whether as chattel or wage slaves. For humans have their own creative power, both as individuals, and collectively in using social power to oppose and resist the intrusions of both capitalism and the state. Anarchist communists from Kropotkin to Bookchin did not seek to abolish power, but sought to ensure that power be both decentralised and instituted in local communities or workers' cooperatives based on direct democracy.

The idea proclaimed by postmodern anarchists (egoists) that power has no "foundations" and is grounded as "nothingness" (Newman 2016: 113) seems to be completely trite and misleading – an example of postmodern anti-realism bordering on nihilism. Of course, as everybody knows power is not a thing but a relationship between social groups (which are certainly not "spooks"). Power therefore has its foundations and basis in human social life and culture, just as human social life has its own grounding in the relationship of humans to the natural (material) world, which has a reality independent of humans.

Power (or politics) is inherent in all social groups (or collectivities) whatever their scale – whether families, kin groups, local communities, economic organisations such as corporations or factories, cultural societies, as well as nation-states and sports clubs. For power is always involved in the order (cooperation), maintenance and management of the group in question, given that individuals (or groups) always have different and often conflicting concerns and interests. The notion that anarchist communists wish to "abolish power", or are "non-political" or express a "non-power" politics (affirmed by the postmodern egoists and rebuked by the Marxists) (see Blackledge 2010: 131, Newman 2016: 47) is quite misleading. For anarchist communists from Kropotkin to Bookchin are not anti-politics, but specifically opposed all forms of hierarchy and power relations. They therefore seek the diffusion and decentralisation of power, and advocate a society – anarchy – based on mutual aid or free association, or what has been described as "horizontal" relations (Milstein 2010: 36). It is thus quite misleading to equate politics with the state – as anthropologists have long been telling us – and Bookchin (2007) indeed makes a clear distinction between democratic politics and what he describes as statecraft.[40]

---

40   **Morris note**: For useful discussions on the nature of power see Bunge 2009: 183-190. Vodovnik 2013: 46-50

The post-anarchist notions that the state does not exist but is rather a "spook", or that we are free, are naïve, idealist sentiments. Nation-states are real social systems and a person imprisoned, or a slave on a slave plantation, or engaged in wage-labour may have autonomy, subjective agency (like other complex life-forms) but they are certainly not free. The conflation of autonomy with freedom (which is a social concept) by postmodern egoists is quite facile.

The Human Subject

Everyone throughout the world and in all human cultures expresses in their thoughts and actions some conception of human nature, and academic philosophers, religious mystics and Stirnerite egoists – the post-anarchists – are no exception. Everyone therefore, whether implicitly or explicitly, articulates some "ontology" of the subject – even though post-anarchists pretend otherwise (Koch 2011). Anarchist communists, specifically Bakunin and Kropotkin (but including also Bookchin, Chomsky and Ward) are accused by post (structuralist) anarchists of allegedly holding an "essentialist" or "humanist" conception of the human subject. This, of course, is to some extent true. For anarchist communists, like everyone else, acknowledge the existence of a universal humanity, namely that all human beings are not only unique individuals, but also species (human) beings. But anarchist communists also recognise that our human identity as an "earthly being", is only one part of a complex understanding of human subjectivity.

"Post-anarchists" tend to express their critique of anarchist communism in two contrasting forms.

The first is to suggest that anarchist communism views the human subject as having a fixed, immutable benign metaphysical essence (May 1994: 63-64, Patton 2000: 8, Newman 2004, Koch 2011).

I have critiqued this misinterpretation of anarchist communism at length elsewhere (Morris 2014B; 178-180, 2014C), emphasising that, as evolutionary naturalists, anarchist communists like Bakunin and Kropotkin, recognised that humans are animals, species-beings, and are thus the product of a long evolutionary history. Human sociality is not therefore some metaphysical essence – as Newman supposes (2004: 113) – but the product of evolution. As many primates, as well as hyenas and badgers, are like humans, social beings, presumably they too have a "benign" essence? Humans are, fundamentally, organisms, earthly beings that have a biological nature. But they do not have some single immutable essence, spiritual or otherwise.

In a discussion of the epistemological basis of anarchism, Andrew Koch outlines the "ontology of the subject" with respect to Godwin, Proudhon and Kropotkin, who all articulate a universalist conception of the human subject. Misleadingly equating representations of human nature (ontology) with state power, Koch chants the fashionable postmodernist mantra that universalism (acknowledging our common humanity) implies "totalitarian politics" (2011: 36). This is quite banal. Radical anti-humanists and anti-universalists like Joseph de Maistre and Adolf Hitler were racists and advocates of totalitarian politics while universalists (humanists) from Godwin and Proudhon to Chomsky and Bookchin are all anarchists and libertarians.

Post-anarchists seem unable to clearly distinguish between empirical facts (people eat cabbages, hence there is such a thing as human nature), social norms (people ought to eat cabbages, as well as respecting and having concern for the integrity and well-being of other humans – humanism), and state laws that are backed by coercive powers (people have to eat cabbages, if they don't they will be subjected to penal sanctions). Anarchist communists are opposed to coercive state power and the ideologies that support it. They are not opposed to empirical facts about the world or social norms, both of which, they freely acknowledge, are intrinsic to the liberty, well-being and self-development of the human individual – Stirner's "unique one".

The second form of critique advanced by the "post" anarchists is to dismiss Bakunin and an earlier generation of anarchists as "modernists", for not only relying on scientific rationality (how awful!) but for holding (allegedly) a "Cartesian concept of human subjectivity" (Call 1999: 100).

The Cartesian notion of the subject, of course, posits the human subject or self as a disembodied rational ego, completely divorced from nature and social life. Conflating Cartesian rationalism with empirical science and Enlightenment humanism – as Lewis Call does – is obfuscating to say the least, while to imply that Bakunin (and other anarchist communists) are "modernists" is completely fallacious. For anarchist communists repudiate all the essential tenets of "modernity" – namely, the capitalist economic system along with private property; the liberal democratic state along with its ideology of nationalism (or state religion); and the whole culture of capitalism, whether expressed in the ultra-rationalism of Cartesian mechanistic philosophy or the possessive individualism (egoism) of bourgeois theorists.

Needless to say, as evolutionary naturalists, both Bakunin and Kropotkin – long before Baudrillard, Lyotard, Lacan, Derrida and other

French intellectuals, hallowed by the postmodern anarchists, repudiated Cartesian philosophy – its mechanistic conception of nature, its dualistic metaphysics and its ontology of the subject which implied, as earlier noted, a transcendental ego outside nature and social life. Post (modern) anarchists completely misunderstand and thus misinterpret both Enlightenment humanism and the evolutionary naturalism of the anarchist communists.[41]

What then is the post-anarchist ontology of the subject, which they pretend not to have? It seems to be largely, as I have stressed above, a re-vamping of Stirner's radical possessive individualism – egoism. The human subject is therefore virtually equated with the ego – the "one" as defined by Stirner. To recall our earlier discussion; for Stirner the ego is the unique individual who seeks to make every material thing, every life-form and every human being into "property". The ego has little or no concern for the integrity and well-being of other humans – indeed any other life form – for they are only viewed as a "means" for the ego's (my) enjoyment and self-development. My "freedom" as an individual is only to the degree that I control as an autocrat and "own" the world (Stirner 1973: 165-

---

41   **Morris note**: On Bakunin's and Kropotkin's evolutionary naturalism and anti-Cartesian metaphysics see McLaughlin 2002, Morris 2004.

170) Stirner's conception of the ego is, to employ his own term, something of a "spook".

Avidly following Stirner, the post-anarchist conception of the human subject, in contrast with the triadic ontology of the anarchist communists (see Morris 2014C), tends to focus entirely on the ego (or self), and is, therefore, one that is narrow, atomistic, abstract and even nihilistic, in that Stirner refers to the social and humanistic (biological) aspects of the human subject as "nothing" to the ego in its "ownness" and "mastery" of the world.

But the human subject is not just an ego but a human organism, not just a singularity but a multiplicity (in both a biological and social sense), not just a unique individual, but also a social, historical, ecological, and above all, a relational being. Our very integrity as a human subject, our self-development and the creation of ourselves as a unique individual (or self) is only meaningful in terms of our relationships with the material world as a species-being (organism) and our relationship with other humans as a social being (person).

But do we really need French academic philosophers to inform us, in obscure jargon, what is perfectly obvious to everyone in all cultures, namely, that the human subject, like other life-forms, is a unique individual? Even dung beetles, cabbages and elephants are "unique ones" or "singularities"!

When in Malawi, for example, I am often addressed by the honorific "father" (bambo) (a social concept); and people may berate someone for their lack of humanity (umunthu, respect for other human beings). According to post-anarchists these would be "fixed" identities, and entail a denial that humans are unique individuals or egos, which therefore risks dealing "violence to singularity" – the unique person (Newman 2016: 39). Both of the above expressions do nothing of the kind, although they intrinsically entail the concepts of society and humanity.

It is clear that Stirner, though expressing a form of possessive individualism (egoism) was an anarchist, opposed to the state, and all structures of social domination, as well as critical of religion and all ideologies that he felt constrained in any way the autonomy of the "unique one". But it is also equally clear that the "egoistic libertarianism" he espoused has been the "ruling ethos" of the powerful throughout human history – whether political tyrants, feudal lords, slave masters, robber barons, or the radical capitalists invoked by Ayn Rand[42] (Bunge 2009: 128). Not surprisingly, anarchist communists have always been critical of the strident egoism (autocracy) expressed by Stirner. As Errico Malatesta wrote:

42   An originator of objectivism whose writings were used as a bedrock for the neoliberal shift of the 1980s.

"If anarchy means non-government, non-domination, how can one call himself an anarchist without lying to himself and others, when he frankly claims that he would oppress others for the satisfaction of his own ego without any scruple or limit, other than that drawn by his own strength. He can be a rebel ... but he sure cannot be an anarchist" (Turcato 2014: 459).

In contrast to the post-anarchists who focus on the possessive ego, anarchist communists, as I have discussed elsewhere in relation to Bakunin and Kropotkin, express a triadic ontology of the human subject (Morris 2014B: 178-180, 2014C). They recognise, like the German Enlightenment philosophers Immanuel Kant and Karl Marx – as well as many contemporary scholars – that human beings always have three distinct but interrelated "natures". These are: as a species being or organism (our human identity), as a social being (or person), and, finally, as a unique individual (or self). As Mario Bunge put it in his definition of human nature – humans are "self-made social animals" (1999: 124).[43]

Human beings are therefore always embedded in, and always creatively engaged with, three

---

43   **Morris note**: On conceptions of human nature as expressed by other radical scholars see Singer 1999, Kovel 2002: 98-104, and Chomsky 2005.

distinct inter-linked historical processes, namely, those of the evolution of humans as a biological species; the socio-historical, which situates the human subject as a person within a specific socio-cultural context (as expressed in various social identities, which in all cultures are multiple, shifting and relational), and, finally, the individual's life history, involving the creative development of a unique self (as distinct from Stirner's possessive ego).

Anarchist communists, as evolutionary naturalists, emphasise, like many contemporary scholars, that humans have a biological nature, and are intrinsically part of the material world. There is, therefore, for anarchists like Bakunin and Bookchin, an essential continuity between natural evolution and human social life and culture (Maximoff 1953: 91, Bookchin 2007). Anarchist communists recognise too, like Erich Fromm and Lewis Mumford, that there is an essential paradox with respect to human life.

As organisms humans have specific causal powers, needs, dispositions and capacities (they can digest meat but not wood!) yet at the same time they are a unique species in having self-consciousness, a deep sociality and a capacity for symbolic culture.

In recent decades, with a resurgence of interest in Darwin and in evolutionary biology, sociobiologists and evolutionary psychologists have reaffirmed (in marked contrast with postmodernist philosophers) a belief in the existence of a universal human nature. They have, however, tended to downplay the fact that humans are socio-cultural beings and express little interest in the existential individual as a unique self. In contrast, anarchist communists, from Bakunin and Kropotkin to Bookchin, strongly affirm that humans not only have a biological nature but are also intrinsically social beings.

Bakunin has emphasised that "man is so much a social animal that it is impossible to think of him apart from society" (Maximoff 1953: 159). Emphasising that humans are both natural and social beings, Bakunin even suggests that humans are not only the most individual of all life-forms but also the most social (Lehning 1973: 136). The relationship between the human individual and society, in all its diverse forms, is, for anarchist communists, one that is complex, dynamic, dialectical, symbiotic and multifaceted. The idea that a human being, as an "ego" (self) is the "enemy" of society) (Parker et al 2011), as I earlier indicated, made no sense at all to anarchists like Bakunin and Kropotkin.

Anarchist communists therefore emphasise that human life could not exist or have any meaning outside of nature and society. The idea of an isolated and solitary individual (or ego), as conceived by liberal ideology, is for anarchist communists a complete abstraction or "fiction".

But what is equally significant is that anarchist communists not only express a "negative" conception of liberty – consisting of a "rebellion" against all forms of coercive authority – but also a positive concept of liberty, that was particularly well expressed by Bakunin who conceived of positive freedom as not only "eminently social" but as entailing the full development and full enjoyment of all human faculties and powers in every person as a unique being or self. As Bakunin wrote, the only freedom truly worthy of the name consists of the "full development of all the material, intellectual and moral powers which are found in the form of the latent capacities in every individual" And every individual is a unique self (Lehning 1973: 196).

Bakunin recognised, like other anarchist communists, that this positive conception of liberty is hardly possible under the yoke of capitalism or within structures of domination, but is only possible in a free society – or what Kropotkin described as "free communism" (Baldwin 1970: 141, Morris 2004: 71). As Bakunin concluded:

"Being free for man (humans) means being acknowledged, considered and treated as such by another man, and by all men around him. Liberty is therefore a feature not of isolation but of interaction, not of exclusion but rather of connection. I myself am human and free only to the extent that I acknowledge the humanity and liberty of all my fellows" (Lehning 1973: 147-48).

Bakunin thus recognised and emphasised the humanity, the sociality and the uniqueness of every human being. But he also recognised that freedom involves more than just the "spirit of revolt" (Kropotkin 1992: 83), for it is essentially a social concept. Bakunin's concept of individuality, like that of other anarchist communists, is not therefore of an isolated ego striving for power and property, but rather a "communal individuality" (Ritter 1980: 3, Morris 2004: 74, Vodovnik 2013: 157).

Social Revolution

Anarchist communists, and most of the radical activists involved in the anti-capitalist protests of recent years, advocate a social revolution, that is, the radical social transformation of existing society – specifically the capitalist economy and all forms of state power. They therefore envisage that "another world is possible" (Fisher and Ponniah 2003). For anarchist communists this would involve the creation of anarchy – an ecological society based on mutual aid, voluntary associations, and truly democratic forms of community self-management.

In complete contrast, postmodern anarchists, whether Nietzschean aristocratic aesthetes (poetic terrorists) (Bey 1999) or Stirnerite egoists (Newman 2016) repudiate the very idea of a social revolution.

The post-anarchist dismissive attitude towards social revolution is hardly a new standpoint. For even prior to the First World War "hard-headed" types (as Malatesta called them) were preaching, given the enormous and growing powers of the modern state, that "revolution is no longer an option" (Turcato 2014: 375).

Rejecting the idea of a social revolution, and lacking any dialectical sensibility, post(modern) anarchists not only erect a radical and completely false dichotomy between insurrectionism (rebellion) and a revolutionary project – social revolution, but also insinuate that revolutionary anarchists do not engage in contemporary issues. Anarchist communists, we are told, apparently lost in utopian dreams of a future "ideal society" are not concerned with the "here and now" and in transforming the present situation (Newman 2016: 12). This, of course, is yet another gross misinterpretation of anarchist communism.

Anarchist communists, as the historical record

shows, have always been involved in local and immediate social and political issues (as well as having global concerns) – whether in relation to labour conditions, housing, land rights, road schemes, nuclear power or the Poll Tax.

An earlier generation of anarchist communists – for example Bakunin, Kropotkin, Goldman, Rocker. Malatesta and Landauer – were all deeply involved in some form of insurrectionary politics – protests, strikes, demonstrations and most significantly in collective struggles against both capitalism and the state (Van der Walt and Schmidt 2009: 20-22). Likewise, more contemporary revolutionary anarchists – who rarely get a mention in post-anarchist texts – anarchists such as Chomsky, Bookchin, Sam Dolgoff, Nicolas Walter, Cindy Milstein and Albert Meltzer[44] – were all radical activists deeply engaged in insurrectionary politics and "here and now" issues – but specifically in collective struggles against both global capitalism and state power.

Setting up a radical dichotomy between insurrectionism (and revolt) – as advocated by post

---

44   Dolgoff (1902-90) was a Russian-born IWW union militant in the US who co-founded the *Anarcho-Syndicalist Review*. Walter (1934-2000) was a British anarchist activist who wrote extensively for *Freedom* newspaper. Milstein is a US social ecologist and board member of the Institute for Anarchist Studies. Meltzer was a British organiser who co-founded the country's Anarchist Black Cross and *Black Flag* newspaper, also writing the well-known memoir *I Couldn't Paint Golden Angels*.

(modern) anarchists – and social revolution as advocated by anarchist communists – is completely misconceived, and facile. For revolutionary anarchists have long recognised that no social revolution is conceivable or possible without the undermining through protests, demonstrations and collective struggle (as well as propaganda) of the hegemony of capitalism and the machinery of the modern state.

Every revolution, whether the French revolution or the Russian revolution, indeed all the major revolutions in the twentieth century (i.e. Spain, Cuba and Iran) were "preceded, triggered and determined" (as Malatesta put it) by "revolts" – protests, strikes, riots, demonstrations, and organised collective struggles of varying scope and intensity. But as Malatesta also emphasised "a revolt is no revolution" (Turaco 1014: 89-93).

Revolts or insurrections, along with wider collective struggles are, for revolutionary anarchists essential for bringing about a revolution – a social revolution. And a revolution for anarchist communists like Kropotkin means the "undermining" or the "overthrowing" of existing capitalist society, along with state power, and replacing it with anarchy.

For anarchist communists anarchy is a free but ordered society – thus one without any structures of government, or hierarchy, or any form of economic explanation. For anarchist communists a social revolution intrinsically involves two interrelated processes or strategies, namely:

1) the undermining of the powers of capitalism and the nationstate,
2) the creation of alternative forms of social life – anarchy – based on mutual aid, involving diverse and complex forms of sociality and voluntary cooperation.

The two processes are interlinked and anarchist communists have always highlighted the fact that when the powers of the state and capitalism have been eroded through revolutionary insurrections, new forms of social life and especially new forms of popular democracy tend to emerge. For example the "sections" in Paris during the French revolution, the workers' soviets (popular assemblies) during the Russian revolution, and the anarchist collectives during the Spanish civil war.[45]

The notion that a social revolution implies the setting up of new structures of coercive power (the revolutionary state), or even new form of sovereignty, is to completely misunderstand and thus again to misrepresent the politics of anarchist communism.

---

45   On these anarchist collectives see Dolgoff 1974, Leval 1975

It is a common pastime among advocates of "post-left anarchy", whether anarcho-primitivists, Nietzschean aristocratic individualists, or Stirnerite egoists (post-anarchists), to conflate the politics of revolutionary anarchists with those of Marxists. But, of course, a social revolution as envisaged by anarchist communists does not involve "storming the winter palace" in order to acclaim the "conquest" of state power (as Trotsky expressed it) but rather the complete opposite: the rejection of all forms of coercive power that inhibit freedom and self-development of the human individual within society.

Revolutionary anarchists have been depicted as viewing society as a single monolithic entity, and as conceiving the social revolution as a single apocalyptic event like the second coming of Christ. Both these views are misleading. Although anarchists like Kropotkin towards the end of the nineteenth century certainly did sense that a social revolution was imminent – a view shared by many of those in power who feared the possibility of a coming revolution – most anarchist communists have recognised that eradicating the capitalist economy and the nation-state that supports it, will be a long and protracted historical process.

What the future holds is unknown, but anarchist communists like Malatesta clearly felt that the "coming revolution" would be a gradual process, and importunately will involve retaining most of the features and institutions of human civilisation that has emerged and developed over the past five thousand years (Turcato 2014). A future society could not thereby imply a return to a hunter-gatherer existence, nor be based simply on a "union of egoists" (which is a contradiction in terms). It would rather entail, as in all existing human societies, complex and enduring social associations – varied social groups and institutions. As in all known human societies, these associations would relate to the four primary spheres of human life-activity, namely, the social (the care and upbringing of children and their education), economic (the production of food, clothing and shelter and the basic necessities of human life), political (institutions relating to the self-management of local communities and forms of confederalism), and, finally the cultural (relating to the arts, sciences and forms of symbolic communication). Those who extol Nietzschean aristocratic free spirits, or acclaim the life of the cynic Diogenes of Sinope, forget that these figures, like religious mystics and the lone ranger, presuppose that other mortals, who tend the earth, will provide them with the basic necessities of human life.

The notion that anarchist communists view "society" as a single, monolithic whole is then a misinterpretation of their social politics. As with most people, anarchist communists like Kropotkin employ the term "society" as a general concept to cover a multitude of different social groups (or social systems) – families, ethnic groups, villages, local communities, factories, schools, nation-states, (which are societies under state rule), cities, economic associations of all kinds, and even social clubs (Kropotkin 1902). The future society that Kropotkin envisages "seeks the most complete development of voluntary association in all its aspects, in all possible degrees for all imaginative aims, ever changing, ever modified, associations which carry in themselves the elements of their durability" (Baldwin 1970: 123).

The idea that anarchist communists view society as a seamless, monolithic entity is therefore entirely misplaced. For Kropotkin the free development of the unique individual as a unique self, and the creation of a society consisting of free association (or voluntary organisations) – a free communism – were dialectically inter-related.

Unlike the post (modern) egoists, Kropotkin and other anarchist communists recognised a person could not be free in an unfree society. As he wrote:

"it is futile to speak of liberty as long as economic slavery exists" – backed by a coercive state (Baldwin 1970: 124).[46]

---

46   **Morris note**: For more see Morris 2004: 70-74

Likewise, setting up a radical dichotomy between "method", ie. the expression of an "anarchist sensibility" (allegedly expressed only by the "new" or "post" anarchists) and "ideology" – the approach of anarchist communists – is also misconceived. Anarchism as a "method" was actually first described by the anarchist communist Malatesta (Turcato 2014: 143), and an "anarchist sensibility" was clearly expressed in the life, writings and political actions of all the early anarchist communists. "Ontological anarchy", as trumpeted by the likes of Bey and Saul Newman is simply the rebranding (for academics) of what Kropotkin long ago described as the "spirit of revolt" (1992: 183), and Malatesta's "sentiment of rebellion". (Turcato 2014: 282). It is largely an academic ploy of putting new labels on old wine bottles! Of course the political actions of the revolutionary anarchists express an "ideology": it is that of anarchist communism as a political theory. But rather than being "non-ideological" the "new" or "post" anarchists articulate their own political ideology – whether anarcho-primitivism, Stirnerite postmodern egoism, Nietzschean aristocratic individualism, or a variety of religious metaphysics.

In Cartesian fashion, typical of liberal (bourgeois) individualists, post (modern) anarchists also make a radical dichotomy between "autonomy" (of the individual) and "democracy". They define democracy as implying the "sovereignty of the people", which is, of course, precisely the ideology of the liberal democratic state. This leads them to view all social groups and institutions whether ethnic peoples, local communities, workers' councils or municipal assemblies as sovereign, and as constituting a "totalising regime of power" (no less!) (Newman 2016: 133). This is not, however, the anarchist communist understanding of direct or participatory democracy. For they do not view society (in its myriad forms), nor people (an ethnic community), nor workers' councils, nor a local community or its assembly, as a "sovereign" social entity. Nor for that matter, do they view the human individual – Stirner's unique one – as sovereign, that is as an autocrat.

For anarchist communists there is no radical dichotomy between a human being as a unique autonomous agent, and society – social life in all its varied forms of community self-management. Anarchist communists recognise, of course, that social life could in some circumstances be oppressive, but they neither advocate nor sanctify the priority of the group over that of the individual. Anarchy, for revolutionary anarchists like Bakunin and Kropotkin, always entails a relationship between the individual and the various social groups and associations to which they belong, as being one that is reciprocal, dynamic and symbiotic, embodying an ethic of complementarity.

One final post-structuralist critique of anarchist communism.

Following Stirner and Nietzsche post (modern) anarchists insinuate that anarchist communists view "reason" and "humanity" as if they were deities. This is best described as nonsense. Reason for anarchist communists is a human faculty or capacity, one among many others, and probably shared to some degree by other social mammals;. It is manifested in symbolic thought, empirical science, and all relational epistemologies. Humanity, for anarchist communists is, of course, a species being, the product, along with human social life and culture, of natural evolution. Only religious anarchists, whether extolling theism, theosophy or transcendentalism, consider humans to be divine beings. Not so anarchist communists.

Post (modern) anarchists like Newman seem oblivious to the recent developments in continental philosophy, which has not only explicitly embraced metaphysics – contrary to Heidegger's so-called "anarchy" – but has reaffirmed ontological realism, the importance of science as a ratio-empirical form of knowledge, and the vitality of philosophical materialism (Bryant et al 2011, Gratton 2014).

All this simply re-affirms the kind of metaphysics – evolutionary naturalism – that was articulated by Bakunin and Kropotkin over a hundred years ago.

Political Strategies

Direct Action

Anarchists – anarchist communists especially – were at the heart of both the anti-globalisation demonstrations[47] and the Occupy movement, and the "spirit of revolt" (as Kropotkin describes it) is at the heart of anarchist communism.

As I have stressed above, anarchy for anarchist communists is fundamentally a social concept, for as many anarchists have indicated over the past century, it can be defined as simply a "society without a ruler". As Malatesta writes:

> "Anarchy is a word that came from the Greeks and signifies, strictly speaking, without government. The state of a people without any constitutional authority that is, "without government" (Turcato 2014: 109).

Anarchy therefore does not mean bombs, violence, disorder or chaos, for as Alexander Berkman insisted:

---

47   The "party and protest" period in Britain broadly started with the Carnival Against Capital in 1999 and continued alongside a worldwide movement of resistance against neoliberal entrenchment throughout the 2000s.

> "It is capitalism and government which stand for disorder and violence Anarchism is the very reverse of it: it means order without government, and peace without violence" (Berkman 1972: 173).

Anarchy, for anarchist communists, thus has a precise meaning; an ordered society without government, or structures of domination and oppression.

In recent decades, however, post-anarchists, that is postmodern egoists (Newman 2016), have rejected this meaning of anarchy and advocated instead three different understandings of the term.

Firstly, as indicated earlier, egoists and Nietzschean aesthetes employ the academic concept "ontological anarchy" as a psychological concept that simply means what generations of anarchists communists have described as "anarchist sensibility" – "the spirit of revolt".

Secondly, given that the Greek term *arche* has a wide range of meaning, referring to origins, first principles or beginnings, as well as rule, postmodern egoists and academics have the gall to describe that arch-reactionary Martin Heidegger as an "anarchist", in that the term "anarchy" is used to depict Heidegger's rejection of metaphysics. But of course, Heidegger was not only an unrepentant fascist and devotee of Adolf Hitler, but (like everybody else!) had his own brand of metaphysics. This is perhaps best described as theological mysticism, with Heidegger yearning for a return, like Himmler, of the neo-pagan "messengers" of the Godhead.

But the third meaning given to anarchy by contemporary postmodern egoists is perhaps more germane to the present discussion. This entails defining and extolling anarchy as meaning disorder, contingency, ephemerality and chaos. This of course reflects the culture of capitalism, as Berkman indicated. This leads the postmodern anarchists, whether mystical Nietzschean individualists (Bey 1991) or radical Stirnerite egoists (Newman 2016), to verily oppose all forms of social organisation, particularly the collective social life of ordinary mortals.

The mutualist Pierre-Joseph Proudhon, of course, famously declared not only that "property is theft", but also that "anarchy is order", for Proudhon recognised as an insightful sociologist, (unlike the postmodern egoists) that all human societies are organised, and that human existence is hardly conceivable without some form of organised social life. In fact, although chance and contingency are intrinsic to earthly existence, the material world itself is not chaotic, for as the Buddha long ago expressed it: everything "arises" from pre-existing conditions. Indeed philosophers of biology have indicated that if the physical world had been chaotic it is difficult to imagine how life itself would ever have emerged.

To reject all social organisation, and to view social life as somehow the "enemy" of the unique ego – as radical egoists contend – seems to me quite facile. Indeed the Russian mystical "anarchist" Nicolas Berdyaev went to an even greater extreme, considering the material world as fundamentally opposed to the "freedom" of the individual!

But here let me digress, for radical egoists, like bourgeois liberals, tend to conflate society with the state, or at least to view social life as inherently involving structures of coercive power.

For many, many years I have been an active member of the Richard Jefferies Society[48]. This society is not a "spook" for it has a material reality and agency, and although not independent of human beings, it is independent of the individual – myself. Indeed the Richard Jefferies Society had been in existence for around half a century before I became a member. Being a member involves obligations and constraints – I have to pay an annual subscription and speak English at meetings – but in no way does it foreclose or inhibit my autonomy. To the contrary, over the

---

48   Jefferies (1848-87) is best known for his writing about nature and the countryside.

years, it has enhanced my own self-development and added to my understanding of the world – particularly the natural world.

Nation-states and capitalist firms – I worked for several years as an employee of Akrill's Iron Foundry in West Bromwich – are, for anarchist communists, very different social forms to that of the Richard Jefferies Society and other voluntary associations. Revolutionary anarchists therefore are not against organisation or social institutions or social groups; they are only opposed to those social forms based on coercive power (states), forms of hierarchy, economic exploitation or cultural oppression. Anarchist communists do not reject social organisation; whether the organisations of working people or local communities in their struggle against capitalism and the state, specific anarchist organisations like, for example, Class War or the Anarchist Federation, or the organisations of everyday social life. The rejection of organisation and social institutions by contemporary Stirnerite egoists is not, however, something new: for even at the end of the nineteenth century – long ago – Malatesta was emphasising the importance of "organisation" against its many detractors in their advocacy of chaos and contingency. The need for organisation in everyday social life, he remarked, is so self-evident that it is "mind-boggling" to think that anyone could doubt it. Significantly, Malatesta emphasises that anarchists "are not out to emancipate the people; we want to see the people emancipate themselves" (Turcato 2014: 233-43).[49] Contrary to the critiques levelled at anarchist communists by postmodern egoists and individualist anarchists, this continues to remain the essential standpoint of revolutionary anarchists. As Benjamin Franks notes:

> "The core of anarchism is that the oppressed themselves carry out their own liberation" (2006: 179).

Interpreting the state as a territorial sovereign institution that monopolises all forms of coercive power and is invariably identified and sanctified by a nationalist ideology – the "god of modernity" as Josep Llobera described it – anarchist communists have always repudiated the state as an agency of social revolution. They have therefore been equally opposed to liberal democracy, the so-called parliamentary road to socialism (reformism), and the Marxist-Leninist approach to political resolution. The latter strategy – the Bolshevik tradition – involves the formation of a strictly

---

49   **Morris note**: For an extended and useful discussion of the various forms of "anti-organisation", which seems to be a recurrent theme within the wider anarchist tradition see Franks 2006: 200-210).

disciplined vanguard party, the "conquest" of state power by the party, and the establishing of a "workers' state" to initiate a socialist revolution.

Ever since Bakunin, anarchist communists have repudiated this conception of radical politics, suggesting that it would inevitably lead to some form of totalitarian rule, and history has proved Bakunin and the early anarchist communists only too prescient.[50]

In being both anti-capitalist and anti-state, and in rejecting all coercive or oppressive forms of authority, the politics of anarchist communism has often been described by the rather obtuse academic term "prefiguration". This simply means a conception of social revolution (or ethics) in which the means of struggle prefigure the aims or objectives of the revolution, namely anarchy. This would be a society based on egalitarian values, a cooperative ethos involving voluntary associations and social solidarity, as well as one which would foster, as Bakunin and Kropotkin stress, the liberty and full development of every human individual as a unique self. As anarchist communists have long emphasised, anarchy means voluntary cooperation, not compulsion or forced participation; "harmony and order in place of interference and disorder" (Berkman 1972: 188).

---

50   **Morris note**: See Berkman 1989, Morris 1996 127-130

Berkman, in fact, expressed the notion of "prefiguration" rather cogently when asked what preparation is needed for the social revolution. He replied:

> "If your object is to secure liberty, you must learn to do without authority and compulsion. If you intend to live in peace and harmony with your fellow-men you and they should cultivate brotherhood and respect for each other. If you want to work together with them for your mutual benefit, you must practise cooperation. The social revolution means much more than the reorganisation of conditions only; it means the establishment of new human values and social relationships" (Berkman 1972: 232, Vodovnik 2013: 188).[51]

The revolutionary anarchist Bookchin, a strong advocate of ethical socialism, succinctly expressed the "prefigurative ethic" when in the closing lines of his well-known polemic he wrote:

> "Listen Marxist! The organisation we try to build is the kind of society our revolution will create" (1971:220) – namely anarchy".

51   **Morris note**: For an extended discussion of the "prefigurative method" (or ethics) see Franks 2006: 97-114

Anarchism, Milstein writes, is first and foremost a "revolutionary political philosophy" offering a fundamental critique of existing society – specifically, the capitalist economy and all forms of state power (Milstein 2010:31). Given that anarchists reject the state as an agency of social revolution, anarchist communists have, therefore, tended to formulate and practise essentially four alternative political strategies, alternative, that is, to political action involving the state. Generally described as direct action, these four strategies are: insurrectionism, anarcho-syndicalism, libertarian politics and community activism.

These are not exclusive strategies, for they overlap in some key respects, but they often tend to be associated with specific anarchists, for example, anarcho-syndicalism with Rocker and Chomsky, and community activism with Colin Ward. I shall discuss each of these social revolutionary strategies in turn. All have one specific aim, namely, the creation of an anarchist society – anarchy.

Such a society, anarchist communists suggest, would be ecological (in harmony with the natural world and other life-forms); libertarian (fostering the liberty and full development of each person as a unique self); socialist (land and all vital resources being held in common); and democratic (involving the self-management of associations and communities, and a confederal political system).

Insurrectionism

Anarchism, anarchist communism especially, as a political tradition, has long been identified with chaos and violence, particularly with "bomb-throwing". For in the early years of anarchist communism, especially around the 1890s, insurrectionism, or what has become known as "propaganda by the deed", was an intrinsic part of the movement. This involved not terrorist acts, but rather the assassination of monarchs and state presidents, or even avenging the deaths of comrades and workers by targeting the individuals held responsible for the bloody repression of striking workers.

But this form of insurrectionism – assassinations – was never more than a minority activity among anarchist communists, although both Malatesta and Berkman were advocates of this form of insurrectionism in their early years. But both men and the movement generally, came to repudiate this form of insurrectionism as a political strategy. The reasons for this are simple: it was held to be elitist, alienating the majority of working people. It was also ineffective, for rather than invoking a social revolution it brought down the wrath of the state and the harsh repression of the whole anarchist communist movement.[52] A social revolution, anarchist communists like Kropotkin came to argue, could therefore only be achieved through a popular movement, or what Van Der Walt and Schmidt (2009: 20-22) describe as "mass anarchism" – collective struggles against both capitalism and the state.

Anarchist communists, however, never rejected what Kropotkin described as the "spirit of revolt" and recognised that insurrectionism in the wider sense – protests, revolts, demonstrations, strikes, occupations, even riots – were an intrinsic part of the struggle against state power and capitalism.

For over a century, liberal politicians and the media generally, whether out of malice, ignorance or as political propaganda, have associated anarchism with violence and bomb-throwing. But as many anarchist texts have emphasised, of all political traditions anarchist communism is perhaps the least violent. Throughout the decades most political assassinations have

---

52   **Morris note**: It is worth emphasising that states do not need any pretext to suppress dissidents, whatever their political aims may be, or radical social movements. As Gelderloos writes: "If the state "wants to repress a movement or organisation, it does not wait for an excuse, it manufactures one" (2007: 57).

nothing to do with anarchists, and almost every political tradition – fascism, liberal democracy, conservatism, nationalism – as well as all religions, have a long and impressive record of direct action in the form of political violence. But what anarchist communists have always strongly emphasised is that all states, all forms of political authority, are based on a monopoly of violence. The main holders and users of bombs, as well as of other forms of violence – as Nicolas Walter emphasised, has not been anarchists but governments. Indeed the origin myths of many nation-states – like that of the United States of America or the French republic – are based on violent acts of rebellion. Equally significant state ceremonials – like that of "Trooping the Colour" in London, are based entirely on the "parade" or "display of military power – the technologies of violence. Finally, most acts of terrorism are state-sponsored.[53]

Unlike many liberal scholars and reformists, who tend to take the violence of the state for granted, anarchist communists have long been concerned with and debated the ethics of political violence – whether in terms of coercive power within a society, or in terms of armed conflict against

---

53   **Morris note:** For useful discussions of anarchism and political violence see Walter 2007:204-44, Dupuis-Deri 2013:52-61, Gelderloos 2007

the state. And as many historians have explored, there are wide differences among anarchists with respect to political violence. These range from the views of Bakunin and Malatesta, who in their early years were directly involved in armed struggles (as later were anarchists in the Spanish Civil War), to the radical pacifism of Leo Tolstoy and the non-violent forms of resistance advocated by many radical liberals.

It is important to recognise that although a distinction may be drawn between insurrectionism and class struggle anarchism (anarcho-syndicalism) as political strategies, both strategies may (or may not) entail acts of violence (Van Der Walt and Schmidt 2009: 143).

Over the past two decades insurrectionism has taken on a new lease of life, not of course in the form of assassinations, but in terms of widespread protests and demonstrations. Anarchist communists have been at the forefront of the various anti-capitalist movements that emerged during this period. With respect to the anti-globalisation demonstrations after Seattle (the so-called "battle of Seattle" took place in November 1999 during a meeting of the World Trade organisation), and the anti-austerity protests and Occupy movement around 2011, it is worth noting that although anarchists were at the "heart" of these demonstrations they were in fact a distinct minority. It is therefore misleading to equate the Occupy movement with anarchism, even though, as I noted earlier, the Occupy movement was deeply influenced by and embraced many of the basic principles of anarchist communism. But, nevertheless, a banner at London Occupy carried the declaration "Reclaim the State" – which is hardly an anarchist sentiment.

It is equally misleading to equate the anarchists involved in the anti-capitalist demonstrations with the so-called "new" or "post" anarchists – whether anarcho-primitivists, anarcho-capitalists, Stirnerite egoists, post-anarchists or Nietzchean poetic terrorists – for class struggle anarchists (those who marshal under such banners as Class War, Solidarity Federation, the anarcho-syndicalist network and the Anarchist (Communist) Federation) were also very much an integral part of the anti-capitalist protests. Insurrectionism – protests and radical activism – has always been intrinsic to anarchist communism, and to class struggle anarchism (Sheehan 2003, Franks 2006).

It is important also to correct the idea that anarchism had been in hibernation since the Spanish Civil War, only to emerge, Phoenix-like from the ashes – as the so-called "new" anarchism during the demonstrations in Seattle in 1999. For anarchist communists had been actively involved in all protests and demonstrated since the Second

World war (and I speak from experience) – against the Vietnam War, against the apartheid system in South Africa, against specific environmental projects, against the proliferation of nuclear weapons, and against the poll tax, as well as against global capitalism. Anarchy alive! (Gordon 2008) – anarchism never actually died.

Anarchist communists have, therefore, been actively involved in insurrectionism – in protests and demonstrations against the state and global capitalism for the better part of the last hundred years (Morris 2014B: 211-212).

Disturbed by the resurgence of anarchism in the 1960s, thirty years before the demonstrations in Seattle, the Marxist historian Eric Hobsbawm was prompted to write his famous essay "Reflections on Anarchism". In the essay Hobsbawm depicted anarchism as a "tragic farce", as having an emotional rather than an intellectual appeal, as a "primitive" form of politics belonging to a pre-industrial age, and he even linked anarchism to the neo-conservative politics of Barry Goldwater (Hobsbaum 1973: 82-91). This says a lot about the limits of Marxist historical scholarship when it comes to discussing anarchist communism.

Anarchist communists have often made distinctions between resistance and radical protest, and between spontaneous riots and planned insurrections. Apart from postmodern egoists and Nietzschean aesthetes like Bey – who seek to detach themselves from the realities of the state and capitalism – for anarchist communists insurrectionism is fundamentally a revolutionary strategy (Bonanno 1988).

But what is novel in the insurrectionary politics of the last decades is the emergence of groupings of radical activists widely known as the black bloc. The black bloc is generally composed of ad hoc groupings of individuals or affinity groups who, at protests and demonstrations, dress in completely black attire with hoods or balaclavas to retain their anonymity. The black bloc was actively involved in all the anti-capitalist protests and demonstrations both during and after the Seattle uprising of popular discontent in 1999. Although sometimes described as "vandals", or as being involved in gratuitous violence, the radical actions of the black bloc – such as smashing windows, pulling down fences, or destroying property – are not mindless acts; they are specifically focused. For their actions "target" the various "icons" of global capitalism, namely, the banks, the high class hotels associated with the political elites, government offices and such emblematic capitalist corporations as McDonalds and Starbucks. The actions of the black bloc are, in fact, a form of "propaganda by the deed", and as political scientist Francis Dupuis-Deri graphically put it, their "target is the message" – corporate capitalism (2013: 66-69). Although often involved in confrontations with the police, the black bloc also played an important role in defending more peaceful protestors from attacks by the police.

Whether pulling down the fences of military establishments or smashing the windows of the Bank of America can be viewed as an "act of violence" is a debatable issue, but nevertheless the destruction of private property and attacks on the police aroused the ire – indeed the outright hostility – of many participants in the anti-capitalist protests. Media figures and radical liberals such as Susan George and George Monbiot were highly critical of the "antics" of the black bloc, for their lack of discipline, their wanton destruction of private property, in upsetting the police (seen as the benign custodians of "law and order"), and in their refusal, as anarchists, to engage in parliamentary politics. The black bloc were thus dismissed as "vandals" and as "unmanageable idiots" (Dupuis-Deri 2013: 115, Morris 2014B 135).

But equally significant, individualist anarchists (or mutualists) as reflected in such periodicals as *The Match* (Fred Woodworth) and *Anchorage Anarchy* (Joe Peacott), emphasising the importance of liberty and private property, and strongly opposed to all forms of violence, were also vehemently opposed to the insurrectionary politics of the black bloc. They were dismissed as uniformed black-clad thugs who disturbed and bullied more peaceful demonstrators.[54]

Insurrectionism as a political strategy, for anarchist communists, embraces not only the kind of actions associated with the black bloc activists, but a diverse variety of tactics that are deemed to question, unsettle and undermine the status quo, state power and the hegemony of neoliberal capitalism that supports it. Such tactics may include peaceful protest marches, reclaiming the streets, sabotage, street theatre, non-violent forms of civil disobedience, sit-ins or occupations and radical environmental protests. Tactical diversity is thus intrinsic to the anarchist communist understanding of insurrectionary politics.

Anarcho-syndicalism

In 1998, shortly before he died, Nicolas Walter published a short, lucid note in the pages of *Freedom* entitled 'The class struggle and anarchism' (2007: 60-62). In it he emphasised that no person ever called themselves an "anarchist" until 1840 – when Proudhon adopted the term

54   **Morris note**: for an informative and sympathetic account of the Black Bloc activists see Dupuis-Deri 2013.

– and that there was no anarchist communist movement until the 1870s.

As I earlier discussed, the anarchist communist movement was essentially founded by the anti-authoritarian sections of the First International, after their split with Marx and the state socialists in September 1872. But Walter also emphasised that the anarchist (communist) movement was most "certainly based on a libertarian version of the concept of the class struggle" (Walter 2007: 61).

Anarchist communism was, therefore, from its conception, a form of class struggle anarchism.

It is common these days among postmodern academics, and some libertarian anarchists, to declare in ocular fashion, that "class" has ceased to have any relevance in the globalisation of capitalism – everything has been reduced to "networks" – and that "class" – along with reason, society and truth – is therefore no longer a valid or useful concept for radical social theory. Two points may be made in this context.

First, capitalism, it is worth insisting, is fundamentally a class system, and all existing nation-states are therefore "divided societies", as Ralph Miliband (1991) long ago emphasised in his study of "class struggle in contemporary capitalism" although, like the autonomous Marxists, Miliband seems singularly unaware – or deliberately ignores – the existence of anarchist communism as a political movement and tradition. All contemporary societies – as nation-states – are therefore class societies, consisting of a dominant class of landowners and capitalists, who own and control capital – specifically land and the means of economic production – and a working class.

The labour of this class, treated as a commodity, is utilised by the ruling class to generate profit, and to accumulate capital. The dominant class draws on the sources of power – the wealth derived from economic exploitation of the working class; the support of the state administration and its coercive apparatus; and finally, the control of the media as a means of communication and persuasion; or as Chomsky put it "the manufacture of consent". The ruling class, the "power elite" themselves, are certainly conscious of their class interests, even if some individualist anarchists and egoists downplay the importance of "class struggle".

Second; it is worth emphasising that rather than the proletariat disappearing with the globalisation of capitalism, there are in fact more industrial workers (along with more sweatshops and forms of economic slavery) in the world today than at any other time in human history. But anarchist communists, ever since Bakunin, rather than focussing exclusively on the proletariat, the industrial worker, as the primary agent of social revolution – as with the Marxists – always expressed a much broader understanding of the working class. For it embraces not only industrial factory workers, but also rural proletarians working on plantations, service workers (in health, education and transport), peasant smallholders and share-croppers, as well as what came to be described as the lumpen proletariat – the marginalised and déclassé elements of modern capitalism. A social revolution, that is, the radical transformation of existing societies, for anarchist communists would therefore necessarily involve working class struggles over a wide range of contexts. In fact, anyone claiming to be "anti-capitalist" is almost, by definition, involved in some form of class struggle.

Engaging in such struggles and social revolution, which entails "creating a free socialist society based on common ownership, self-management and democratic planning from below, and production for need not profit" (Van Der Walt and Schmidt 2009: 6) – has always been fundamental to anarchist communists. Only in such a society, what Kropotkin called "free communist", is freedom, the liberty (autonomy) and full development of the individual as a unique person, truly possible. There is no freedom within capitalism whatever egoists may think or pretend.

Anarcho-syndicalism has therefore always been a key political strategy for anarchist communists.

It is, however, quite misleading to erect a radical dichotomy between anarchist communism and anarcho-syndicalism, as do many anthologies of anarchist writings. For anarchist communism is not a strategy but a political movement and philosophy, and most anarchist communists have championed anarcho-syndicalism as a form of direct action (Van Der Walt and Schmidt 2009: 124-27).

It is worth emphasising that many revolutionary syndicalists like Elizabeth Gurley Flynn, William "Big Bill" Haywood and Daniel De Leon, were not anarchists, instead tending to describe themselves as Marxists, and thus statists. Even so many anarchists, specifically Stirnerite egoists and individualist anarchists (mutualists), repudiated anarcho-syndicalism as a political strategy and the very idea of workers going on strike is almost anathema to the individualists.

Anarcho-syndicalism, or class struggle anarchism, essentially emerged among the followers of Bakunin, the "federalist" sections of the First International and besides Kropotkin and Malatesta, most anarchist communists became fervent advocates. These include, for example, the French syndicalists Emile Pouget and Fernand Pelloutier and later the Spanish anarchists Gaston Leval and Jose Peirats (Damier 2009 Ealham 2015). But a key figure in the development of anarcho-syndicalism was Rudolf Rocker whose text *Anarcho-Syndicalism* (1989) has become something of an anarchist classic.

Anarcho-syndicalism is a form of libertarian socialism – as a political strategy – that attempts to combine an emphasis on class struggle and the emancipation of the working class, with anarchist principles being fundamentally anti-state and anti-capitalist. As it developed in the early years of the twentieth century it had the following characteristics.

First, it repudiated entirely the anarchic tactic of "propaganda by the deed", specifically acts against the bourgeois state involving individual assassinations of presidents, monarchs or leading capitalists.

Second, it critiqued and rejected the parliamentary road to socialism as advocated by the British Labour Party, the German Social Democrats and various other socialist parties. This, for anarcho-syndicalists, would simply lead to reform within the capitalist system, which would remain intact.

Finally, the anarcho-syndicalists as anarchist communists repudiated entirely the Marxist conception of the "dictatorship of the proletariat" through a revolutionary vanguard party and its "conquest" of state power (as discussed above).

Anarcho-syndicalists like Rocker clearly felt that the parliamentary road to socialism would simply lead to the disempowering of the working class, while the seizure of state power by a revolutionary communist party, as with the Bolsheviks, would lead to bureaucratic state capitalism (Rocker 1989: 85, Morris 2014B: 160).

Anarcho-syndicalism therefore put a fundamental emphasis on the class struggle, and on the role of the trade unions and the workers associations, which were conceived as having a dual function.

On the one hand, the unions were to defend and improve workers' rights, wages and living conditions in the present day – as reforms from below. On the other hand the unions were to be the means of completely re-constructing social life through direct actions, workers' solidarity and self-management, and through federal principles. The anarcho-syndicalists contended that the trade unions or syndicates, through engaging in class struggle, would become the "embryo" of a future socialist society. As Rocker put it:

"The trade union, the syndicate, is the unified organisation of labour and has for its purpose the defence of the interests of the producers within existing society, and the preparing for and practical carrying out of the reconstruction of social life after the pattern of socialism" (1989: 86).

Rocker bewailed the fact that the Bolsheviks in their fanatical zeal for government had completely betrayed the social revolution in Russia (1989: 95).

But Rocker and the anarcho-syndicalists did not reject other forms of direct action, whether insurrectionism, in the form of sabotage, boycotts, or strikes, especially the general strike and anti-militarist propaganda or actions, or community-based direct actions or activities.

Contrary to the critiques of the "new" anarchists, Rocker and other anarcho-syndicalists did not see any contradiction between class struggle – opposing capitalism and other forms of hierarchy and state power – and advocating mutual aid, autonomous communities, voluntary associations and workers' self-management.

Anarcho-syndicalism as a political strategy has not been without its critics. Long ago Errico Malatesta, although never abandoning the class struggle, emphasised that trade unions often had a tendency to become bureaucratic organisations, and in seeking recognition of the state and capitalist proprietors, in adapting to existing economic conditions, they often lost the "revolutionary impulse" or the "spirit of revolt" that was intrinsic to anarchist communism. It is quite misleading, Malatesta stressed, to equate syndicalism with anarchism, or to view anarcho-syndicalism as the only "means" we have for the "realisation" of an anarchist society (Turcato 2014: 337-342).

Both Kropotkin and more recently Bookchin also emphasised the limitations of anarcho-syndicalism as an exclusive political strategy. Although acknowledging the necessity of participating in or engaging with the working class movement, and supporting workers and peasants in their struggles against capitalism and the state, it was narrow and limiting, both men felt, to focus exclusively on the factory system and on the general strike. It is, however, fair to note that anarcho-syndicalists – for example, Rocker, Gregori Maximoff[55], Dolgoff and Meltzer – had a fairly broad conception of anarchist communism, and they certainly did not believe that a general strike would bring down the capitalist system "in a few days" (Rocker 1989: 121). The anarcho-syndicalists also recognised the importance of the Spanish (social) revolution as an exemplification of libertarian socialism in action.

Anarcho-syndicalism – as expressed in the principles of revolutionary syndicalism drafted by the International Workers' Association in 1922[56] –

---

55   Maximoff (1893-1950) was a Russian-born organiser involved with Ukrainian anarcho-syndicalist movement Nabat. His book *The Guillotine at Work: Twenty Years of Terror in Russia* charts the Bolsheviks' repression of Russia's anarchist movement.

56   Not to be confused with the International Working Men's Association (the First International) the IWA of the 1920s was the

maintains that the social and economic monopolies intrinsic to capitalism must be replaced by a free, self-managed federation of agrarian and industrial workers united in a system of unions.

As such anarcho-syndicalism is largely focused around economics and therefore tends to bypass struggles specifically focused around the local community or the municipality (or the city as a bioregion). Thus I turn now to two contrasting forms of direct action – the political strategies of libertarian politics, and community activism. But nevertheless it is worth emphasising that anarcho-syndicalism is still a flourishing and worldwide movement, reflected in such radical magazines as *Black Flag* (London), *The Rebel Worker* (Sydney) and *the Anarcho-Syndicalist Review* (Philadelphia).

It certainly remains one of the main "currents" of contemporary anarchism in Britain (Franks 2006: 162, Christie and Meltzer 2010).

Libertarian Politics

To many Stirnerite egoists and individualist anarchists, the very idea of "libertarian politics" is

---

largest anarcho-syndicalist federation in history involving the Spanish, CNT, Germany's FAUD, USI in Italy etc. It was largely destroyed by the rise of fascism.

a contradiction in terms. But as Rocker insisted, politics is intrinsic to social life, for every event that affects the life of a community is of a political nature (1989: 115).

Many anarchists, among whom Bookchin has been the most vocal, have been highly critical of anarcho-syndicalism, given it's over emphasis on the economy and on workers' control. As an alternative political strategy Bookchin therefore sought to develop political institutions, as a counter power to both global capitalism and the nation state.

In response to the social and ecological crisis that now confronts humanity, Bookchin not only reaffirmed the need to develop a philosophy of evolutionary (dialectical) naturalism and an ecological sensibility, he also stressed the need to create – as an alternative to liberal capitalism – an ecological society that was not only in harmony with the natural world, but that was also libertarian, socialist and democratic.

Bookchin, of course, always acknowledged the importance of protests and struggles to achieve a better world – whether centred on nuclear power, ecological issues, health care and education, or on community issues, as well as stressing the importance of the anti-globalisation movement in challenging capitalism, both on cultural and economic grounds (Bookchin 2007: 85).

Like Malatesta, though often critical of anarcho-syndicalism as a political strategy, Bookchin always strongly affirmed the centrality of class struggle. In contrast to such modern media figures as Naomi Klein, Susan George and George Monbiot, who yearn for a benign form of liberal capitalism, Bookchin was always stridently anti-capitalist. Not humanity, but capitalism is responsible for the ecological crisis, Bookchin always stressed.

In contrast to the Marxists, the anarcho-syndicalists and those he described as "lifestyle anarchists" (discussed above) – that is the Stirnerite egoists, Nietzschean mystical aesthetes, existentialists, and anarcho-primitivists – Bookchin aimed to develop and articulate, within the political tradition of anarchist communism, a new form of libertarian politics. It was a form he felt that was implicit in the early writings of both Bakunin and Kropotkin – the democratic self-management, through assemblies, of the community or municipality.

Always eager to develop and promote libertarian municipalism as an integral part and as the political dimension of anarchist communism (communalism) Bookchin, in his extensive writings, described the many forms of popular assemblies that had emerged during the course of European history, particularly during times of social revolution. Bookchin was particularly enthusiastic with regard to the ancient Athenian polis and the system of direct democracy – though he recognised its historical context and limitations. But forms of popular democracy have occurred throughout human history, and, like Kropotkin, Bookchin describes in particular, the popular assemblies of medieval towns, the neighbourhood sections during the French revolution, the Paris commune of 1871, the workers' soviets during the Russian revolution, and the New England town meetings, as well as the anarchist collectives during the Spanish civil war in the late 1930s (Bookchin 1992, 2007: 49).

Unlike Nietzschean "free spirits" and Stirnerite "egoists", who in elitist fashion rely on other mortals to provide them with the basic necessities of life, Bookchin recognised – like other anarchist communists mentioned above – that throughout human history some form of social organisation has always been evident, for humans are intrinsically social beings, not autonomous possessive egos (or autocrats). Some kind of organisation has therefore always been essential not only in terms of human survival, but specifically in terms of the care and bringing up of children (kinship); in the production of food, shelter and clothing and the basic necessities of social life (social economy); and, finally, in the management of human affairs, relating to community decisions and to the resolution of conflicts (politics). Bookchin, therefore, was always keen to distinguish between ordinary social life – focused around family life and kinship, affinity groups, various cultural associations and productive activities – and the political life of a community focused around local assemblies.

Bookchin was equally insistent on distinguishing between politics – which he defined as a theory relating to a public realm and those social institutions by means of which people democratically manage their community affairs – and what he called statecraft. The latter is focused on the state as a form of government that serves as an instrument for class exploitation and for class oppression and control.

Bookchin thus came to put a focal emphasis on the need to establish popular democratic assemblies based on the municipality, on neighbourhoods, towns and villages. Such local assemblies, through face to face democracy, would make policy decisions relating to the management of community affairs.

He argued consistently that such decisions should be made through majority vote, though Bookchin does not advocate majority rule, and emphasised that a free society could only be one that fosters the fullest degree of dissent and liberty. He was therefore always sceptical of consensus politics, except in relation to small groups. Municipalities would be linked through a confederal political system. Although Stirnerite egoists and anarcho-primitivists have always accused anarchist communists like Kropotkin and Bookchin of advocating the formation of "city states", Bookchin always warned of the dangers of any assembly becoming an "incipient state" (Bookchin 1971: 168, 2007: 101-110).

Bookchin summed up his own conception of anarchist politics in terms of four basic tenets:

> ".. a confederation of decentralised municipalities; an unwavering opposition to statism; a belief in direct democracy; and a vision of a libertarian communist society (Bookchin 1995B: 60).

Many anarchists, both individualist anarchists (Joe Peacott) and anarcho-syndicalists (Graham Purchase) have been highly critical of Bookchin's strident advocacy of libertarian municipalism. They have emphasised that Bookchin's stress on politics and citizenship led him to neglect the importance of class and the economic aspects of social life, especially workers' cooperatives; that in harshly critiquing the individualism of the "lifestyle" anarchists, though valid, Bookchin tends to go to the other extreme and virtually downplays the libertarian and "lifestyle" aspects of cultural life that he had extolled in his early writings; and finally, that Bookchin makes too stark a dichotomy between anarcho-syndicalism and community politics, in that early anarchist communists, especially Bakunin and Kropotkin, advocated both anarcho-syndicalism and the "free federation of communities" – the local assemblies (Van Der Walt and Schmidt 2009: 124-26, Morris 2014B:170).

Community Activism

Peter Kropotkin once remarked that within British political culture there existed three great movements of radical politics that were largely independent of the state, and augured well for a social revolution. These were the trade union movements, municipal socialism and the vibrant tradition of voluntary organisation (Rocker 1989: 105).

It is this last movement which forms the basis of the final political strategy of anarchist communism, that of community activism which may in fact take many forms. It is what Colin Ward (1973) described as *Anarchy in Action*. It essentially involves ordinary people "acting for themselves" (as Kropotkin put it), taking full control over their own lives, and through "direct action" establishing their own associations and groups, independent of both the state and capitalism. It may involve squatting or establishing housing associations; the creation of food co-ops, affinity groups or independent free schools; or simply organising campaigns around environmental or community issues. The emphasis is on establishing voluntary associations that enhance peoples' autonomy and reduce their dependence on the state and capitalist corporations.

Ever since Kropotkin, anarchist communists have emphasised community activism, and stressed the importance of voluntary associations and mutual aid societies, some fleeting and ephemeral, others enduring, relating to the many different spheres of social life – social, economic, political and cultural (artistic and intellectual) (Baldwin 1970: 132). Kropotkin was fond of quoting the Lifeboat Association as an example of a spontaneous and enduring social organisation that was independent of the state, and was motivated by mutual aid, and not by the exploitation of others.

Indeed Ward defined anarchism as a social and political philosophy – anarchist communism – that emphasised the natural and spontaneous tendency of humans to associate together for their mutual benefit. Anarchism is thus the idea "that it is possible and desirable for society to organise itself without government" (Ward 1973: 12). Direct action within the community is something that is positive and is not to be equated, as some anarchists do, with insurrectionism – with, that is, sabotage and violent confrontations with the police (state) over a building or piece of land that has "iconic" links with the capitalist system. Many community activists, as well as individualist anarchists (as noted above) have been critical of the tactics of black bloc, feeling that it is an ineffective strategy given the enormous powers of the modern state,

But as an advocate of community activism as a political strategy Ward had little time for self-indulgent hippies – the Hakim Beys of the 1960s – who simply wanted to isolate or detach themselves from the realities of capitalism and the authoritarian state. As a disciple of Kropotkin and Gustav Landauer, Ward wanted to radically transform the structure of contemporary society, and though critical of Kropotkin's "overly optimistic" conception of social revolution, and the idea that the state could simply be "smashed" through insurrectionary tactics alone, Ward followed his mentors Kropotkin and Landauer in advocating social revolution.

He was fond of quoting the well-known sentiments of Landauer who was critical of those ...

"... who regard the state as a thing or fetish that one can smash in order to destroy it. The state is a condition, a certain relationship among human beings, a mode of behaviour between men; we destroy it by contracting other relationships, by behaving differently towards one another" (Lunn 1973: 226, Ward 1973: 19).

Ward also often used the metaphor of the "seed beneath the snow", to suggest the kind of anarchist strategy that would enhance and develop all forms of mutual aid and voluntary cooperation within a community, small-scale initiatives that in some way undermined or bypassed all forms of authority and the power of capitalism.

Ward has often been described as either a precursor of the "new" or "lifestyle" individualism, or as a wishy washy radical liberal. But these interpretations are misleading, for Ward explicitly and firmly situated himself in the revolutionary socialist tradition of Proudhon, Kropotkin and Landauer. He was essentially a social anarchist who, as I have described elsewhere, creatively and insightfully developed the anarchist communist legacy of Kropotkin, making it relevant to contemporary social issues (Levy 2013: 72-87).

The anarcho-syndicalist Albert Meltzer unfairly dismissed Ward as a "bourgeois intellectual" and as a "failed mandarin", and as the "inspiration" for the anarcho-capitalism that emerged during the Thatcher era (Meltzer 1996: 322). This view is seemingly endorsed by Benjamin Franks (2006: 57) who portrays Ward as simply a radical liberal concerned only with protest, not with social revolution.

Ward, of course, never attempted to be a "mandarin", if by that term one means a state functionary, and it seems rather strange to describe someone like Ward, who viewed himself as a "propagandist" for anarchism, and who was opposed to both state power and capitalism – as a "bourgeois liberal".[57]

The main point of course, is that Ward endorsed only one of the political strategies of anarchist communism – that of community activism – and seems to have virtually ignored other forms of direct action – insurrectionism (Bonanno), anarcho-syndicalism (Rocker, Meltzer) and libertarian politics (Bookchin).

All four strategies, of course, are intrinsic to anarchist communism, are interrelated, and were advocated by Kropotkin and the early revolutionary socialists. They are interrelated in the sense that only through insurrectionism

---

57   **Morris note**: For a more balanced approach to the life and thought of Colin Ward see Levy 2013

(protests, demonstrations) and class struggle politics can autonomous spaces be opened up for libertarian politics and community activism. As Peter Gelderloos[58] has indicated, acting for ourselves and building alternative forms of social life within a community is only one half of the equation. We need also to challenge and destroy "existing institutions, and (defend) ourselves and our autonomous spaces in the process" (Gelderloos 2007: 98).

It is, then, important to recognise that anarchist communism advocates a plurality of political strategies which become relevant in relation to the interests and personalities of specific anarchists, as well as in relation to the different socio-historical conditions in which individuals and their associations find themselves. For example, while in his early years Rocker was a strong advocate of anarcho-syndicalism, in his final years he was more involved in community politics – though many regretted Rocker's support of the Allies in the Second World War.

But importantly in struggles against the state and capitalism and in creating alternative forms of social life based on voluntary associations and self-managed communities, all four political strategies are involved and necessary.

---

58   Gelderloos is the author of a number of noted modern works including *How Nonviolence Protects the State* and *Anarchy Works*.

Epilogue

In this book I have attempted to offer, within a wide-ranging and critical survey of several other radical traditions, an introduction to anarchist-communism. I have explored its origins as a social movement at the end of the nineteenth century, its basic principles as a political ideology. And I have defended its integrity and importance against the critique and misrepresentation of its detractors – mainly recent devotees of post-structural theory. I have also discussed its political praxis, the various forms of direct action that are intrinsic to anarchist communism as a political philosophy. These are insurrectionism, anarcho-syndicalism, libertarian politics and community activism,

But to conclude this book I will offer four final reflections.

First, the "new" or "post" anarchists (egoists), following in the wake of the postmodern theorists (Nietzsche and Heidegger especially) tend to make a radical dichotomy between life (action) and thought (ideology) and then to not only denigrate ideas – along with reason and theory – but to make an absolute fetish of "action". Anarchist communists are, therefore, quite perversely identified with ideas (ideology) not with action. This dichotomy is, I think, not only misleading but completely obfuscating. For life (action) without thought, is a life without meaning (nihilism). But for human beings, as for all other animals, life – involving our interactions with the material world – is inherently meaningful. As one anthropologist graphically put it, there are indeed "signs of meaning" in the universe. The triumph of the "will" over the intellect has rather disturbing parallels. Claiming to be "non-ideological" (devoid of ideas?), or following Martin Heidegger in proclaiming the "closure" of metaphysics as the post-anarchists (egoists) do, seems to me to verge on sophistry. Anarchist communists of course have always emphasised the importance of both life and thought, direct action and reflective theory.

It is therefore somewhat ironic that the "post truth" scenario of Heidegger and the "post" anarchists – as Stirner put it "you alone are the truth" (1973: 350) – is particularly well expressed in the autocratic politics of that arch-egoist Donald J. Trump.

Second, the "new" or "post" anarchists – whether egoists, religious anarchists, or Nietzschean aesthetes (or their academic supporters) – always pride themselves as being creative, experimental, innovative, non-ideological, and flexible, and as expressing an authentic anarchist sensibility, the "spirit of revolt" (ontological anarchy).

In contrast anarchist communists are depicted, and continually rebuked and denigrated by these "new" and "post" anarchists for being dogmatic, authoritarian, ideological, sectarian, confrontational, inflexible, as well as lacking in an anarchist "spirit" or sensibility. They are also admonished for making a "fetish" of the state. This negative portrait is a complete caricature of the life, thoughts and political praxis of generations of anarchist communists past and present (Morris 2014B: 185-186). No wonder Bookchin expressed his despair that his firm commitment for anarchist values and principles was denounced as "dogma"; that his support for revolution over reformism was condemned as "sectarian"; and that his fervent defence of anarchist communism – as against primitivism, egoism and mysticism – was castigated as "authoritarian"!

But what do the "new" or "post" structuralist anarchists have to offer that is "innovative" and "experimental"? What do they tell us will "revitalise" anarchism? As far as I can tell three strategic moves are advocated by the "new anarchists", all of which, from an anarchist communist perspective are highly problematic.

The first is to revamp the bourgeois individualism of the nineteenth century, either by invoking Stirner's radical egoism and insurrectionism (ontological anarchy), or by conceiving of a "society without a state" as implying some form of anarcho-capitalism (libertarian anarchy). Both ideologies are a long way from Kropotkin and Malatesta's conceptions of libertarian socialism.

The second innovation of the "new" or "post" anarchists is to completely abandon the evolutionary naturalism that has been developing over the past two centuries. This is a materialist philosophy that embraces a realist conception of being, a rational-empiricist approach to how we experience reality and a form of ethical naturalism. It was a philosophy that was affirmed by many anarchist communists as the metaphysical "grounding" of their class struggle politics. This is now rejected, and in its place we are urged by the "new" anarchists to adopt – put our faith in – some rather dated religious metaphysic. As I discussed in Section Two, a variety of religious traditions have been extolled: neo-paganism, Christianity, Islamic mysticism, theosophy (panentheism) and transcendentalism.

Alternatively, we are urged to embrace modern nihilism, the culture of global capitalism with its emphasis on fragmentation, chaos, contingency and ephemerality. This step is atavistic rather than new or innovative.

Third, perhaps even more innovative (sic), anarchist communists are now being urged to abandon their rigid opposition to the state.

Chomsky, for example, affirms the need for "strengthening" the liberal state – the US federal government no less – in order to curb the "predations" of capitalist corporations. Following Chomsky, Vodovnik writes:

> "To pursue ideals such as freedom and equality, today's anarchists should defend the state against the attacks of multinational capitalism" (2013: 49).

But for anarchist communists the state and capitalism have a close symbiotic relationship, and to reject Ayn Rand's neoliberal capitalism certainly does not imply embracing the liberal democratic state.

As a third reflection it is worth noting that anarchist communists are often berated, especially by eclectic religious anarchists, for being sectarian as social anarchists. They pride themselves in advocating an "anarchism without adjectives". They neglect to mention that the term "anarchism without adjectives" was coined by Malatesta and his associates in the 1890s to denote anarchist communism. For in critiquing those who described themselves as individual anarchists, Malatesta strongly affirmed that anarchist communists were both libertarian (individualist) and socialist.

Finally, it is important to recognise and stress the vitality and continuing relevance of anarchist communism as a political tradition. Like all social movements, anarchist communism is complex, diverse, and ever-changing, open and responding to new events and new ideas, creatively adapting over the years to the globalisation of capitalism and the increasing incursions of the modern state into almost every aspect of social life.

Yet at a time when global capitalism seemingly reigns triumphant, and is virtually unchallenged by all the main political parties, and we are facing a crisis of unprecedented scope, we surely need to take seriously the political legacy of anarchist communism. For the "modern crisis", as Bookchin contended, is indeed manifold – social, economic, political and ecological.[59]

Yet in terms of this crisis, all the political traditions that now dominate the contemporary political landscape – liberal democracy in its various forms; neo-conservatism, including its offspring, authoritarian populism; Marxism; and theocracy, as expressed in various forms of religious fundamentalism – are virtually politically bankrupt, and have little to offer that ray of "social hope" that the liberal philosopher Richard Rorty yearned for.

---

59   **Morris note**: I have described this crisis at length in my study of Kropotkin 2004: 14-17.

References

Adam, J.P 1992 *Reformist Anarchism. A Study in the Feasibility of Anarchism* Braunton: Merlin Press

Baldwin, R.N. (Ed) 1970 *Kropotkin's Revolutionary Pamphlets* New York: Dover

Barclay, H. 1982 *People Without Government* London: Kahn and Averill

Belsey, C. 1980 *Critical Practice* London: Methuen

Berdyaev, N. 1943 *Slavery and Freedom* London: Centenary Press

Berkman, A. 1972 *What is Communist Anarchism?* (original 1928) New York: Dover 1989 *The Bolshevik Myth* (original 1925) London: Pluto Press

Berry, D. 2009 *A History of French Anarchism Movements* 1917-1945 Oakland. Ca: AK Press

Bey, H. 1991 *Taz: The Temporary Autonomous Zone, Ontological Anarchism Poetic Terrorism* Brooklyn, NY: Automedia

Biehl, J. 1988 *The Politics of Social Ecology: Libertarian Municipalism* Montreal: Black Rose Books

Blackledge, P. 2010 *Marxism and Anarchism International Socialism* 125: 131-159

Bollier, D. 2014 *Think Like a Commoner* Gabriola Is: New Society Publications

Bonanno, A.M. 1988 *From Riot to Insurrection* London: Elephant Editions

Bookchin, M. 1971 *Post-Scarcity Anarchism* (1974 edition) London: Wildwood House 1982 *The Ecology of Freedom* Palo Alto: Cheshire 1989 *Remaking Society* Montreal: Black Rose Books 1992 *Urbanization Without Cities: The Rise and Decline of Citizenship* (original 1987) Montreal: Black Rose Books 1995 *A Re-Enchanting Humanity* London: Cassell 1995 *Social Anarchism or Lifestyle Anarchism :An Unbridgeable Chasm* San Francisco: AK Press 2007 *Social Ecology and Communalism* Oakland, Ca. AK Press

Brown, L.S. 1993 *The Politics of Individualism* Montreal: Black Rose Books

Bryant, L., N. Srnicek and G. Harman (Eds) 2011 *The Speculative Turn: Continental Materialism and Realism* Melbourne: Repress

Bufe, C. and M. Verter (Eds) 2005 *Dreams of Freedom: The Ricardo Flores Magon Reader* Edinburgh: AK Press

Bunge, M. 1996 *Finding Philosophy in Social Science* New Haven: Yale University Press 1999 *Dictionary of Philosophy* Amherst, NY: Prometheus Press 2009 *Political Philosophy: Fact, Fiction and Vision* New Brunswick: Transaction Call, L. 1999 *Anarchy in the Matrix* Anarchist Studies 7/2: 99-117 2002 *Postmodern Anarchism* Lanham: Lexington Books

Carroll, J. 1974 *Break-out From the Crystal Palace* London: Routledge and Kegan Paul

Casey, G. 2012 *Libertarian Anarchy: Against the State* London: Bloomsbury

Chomsky, N. 2005 *Chomsky on Anarchism* Ed.B. Pateman Edinburgh AK Press

Christie, S. and A. Meltzer (Ed) 2010 *The Floodgates of Anarchy* (original 1970) Oakland, Ca: PM Press

Clark, J.P. 1976 *Max Stirner's Egoism* London: Freedom Press 2013 *The Invisible Community: Realising Communitarian Anarchism* London: Bloomsbury

Cole, G.D.H. 1954 *A History of Socialist Thought: Vol 2 Marxism and Anarchism 1850-1890* London: MacMillan

Cudenec, P. 2013 *The Anarchist Revelation* Sussex: Winter Oak Press

Damier 2009 *Anarcho-Syndicalism in the 20th Century* Edmonton: Black Cat Press

Davis, A.T 2003 *Are Prisons Obsolete?* New York: Seven Stories Press

Deleuze, G. and F. Guattari 1977 *Anti-Oedipus: Capitalism and Schizophrenia* (original 1972) New York: Viking Press

Detmer, D. 2003 *Challenging Postmodernism Philosophy and the Politics of Truth* Amherst: Humanity Books

Dolgoff, S. 1974 *The Anarchist Collectives: Workers' Self-Management in the Spanish Revolution 1936-1939* New York Freelife Editions

Dupuis-Deri, F. 2013 *Who's Afraid of the Black Bloc: Anarchy in Action*

Around the World (original 2007) Oakland, Ca. PM Press

Ealham, C. 2015 *Living Anarchism: Jose Peirats and the Spanish Anarcho-Syndicalist Movement* Oakland, Ca. AK Press

Ellen, R. 1986 What Black Elk Left Unsaid *Anthropology Today* 2/16:8-12

Eltzbacher, P. 1900 *Anarchism: Exponents of the Anarchist Philosophy* (Ed J.Martin 1958 edition) New York: Chips Book Store

Fisher, W.F and T. Ponniah (eds) 2003 *Another World is Possible: Popular Alternatives to Globalization* London: Zed Books

Foucault, M. 1970 *The Order of Things: The Archaeology of the Human Sciences* (original 1966) London: Tavistock 1977 Language, *Counter-Memory, Practice: Selected Essays and Interviews* Ithaca: Cornell University Press

Franks, B. 2006 *Rebel Alliances: The Means and Ends of Contemporary British Anarchism*. Oakland, Ca. AK Press

Gelderloos, P. 2007 *How Non-Violence Protects the State* Cambridge, Mass: South End Press

Gellner, E. 1992 *Postmodernism, Reason and Religion* London: Routledge

Giddens, A. 1998 *The Third Way* Cambridge: Polity Press

Gordon, V. 2008 *Anarchy Alive* London: Pluto Press

Graham, R. 2015 *We Do Not Seek Anarchy, We Invoke It* Oakland, Ca. AK Press

Graeber, D. 2013 *The Democracy Project* London: Penguin Books

Gratton, P. 2014 *Speculative Realism: Problems and Prospects* London: Bloomsbury

Harris, M. 1995 Anthropology and Postmodernism in M.F. Murphy and M. Margous (Eds) *Science, Materialism and the Study of Culture* Gainesville: University Press of Texas pp 62-77

Herman, E. and N. Chomsky 1988 *Manufacturing Consent: The Political Economy of the Mass Media* New York: Pantheon

Hobsbawm, E. 1973 *Revolutionaries: Contemporary Essays*. London: Quartet Books

Holloway, J. 2002 *Change the World Without Taking Power* (2005 edition) London: Pluto Press

Hopton, T. 2010 Tolstoy, History and Non-Violence *Anarchist Studies 18/2*: 19-28

Horowitz, I.L. (Ed) 1964 *The Anarchists* New York: Dover

Jameson, F. 1998 *The Cultural Turn: Selected Writings on Postmodernism* London: Verso

Job, S. 2016 Bakunin and the Entheogenic Challenge to Atheism *Anarchist Studies 24/2*: 83-105

John, W. 1995 *Christianity: A Primer in Christian* Anarchism Brighton: Black Cat Publications

Joll, J. 1964 *The Anarchists* London: Methuen

Jun, N. 2011 Reconsidering Post-Structuralism and Anarchism in D. Rousselle and S. Evren (Eds) (2011) pp 231-49

Kinna, R. 2005 Anarchism: A Beginner's Guide Oxford: Oneworld Publications

Koch, A.M. 2011 *Poststructuralism and the Epistemological Roots of Anarchism* in A. Rouselle and S.Evren (Eds) (2011) pp 23-40

Kovel, J. 2002 *The Enemy of Nature: the End of Capitalism or the End of the World* London: Zed Books

Kropotkin, P. 1902 *Mutual Aid: A Factor in Evolution* (1939 edition) London: Penguin Books 1985 *Act for Yourselves* London: Freedom Press 1992 *Words of a Rebel* Montreal: Black Rose Books 1993 *Fugitive Writings* Montreal: Black Rose Books

Lehning, A. 1973 *Michael Bakunin: Selected Writings* London: Cape

Leval, G. 1975 *Collectives in the Spanish Revolution* London: Freedom Press

Levy, C. (ed) 2013 *Colin Ward: Life, Times and Thought* London: Lawrence and Wishart

Lovejoy, A. and G.Boas 1935 *Primitivism and Related Ideas in Antiquity* Baltimore: J.Hopkins University Press

Lunn, E. 1973 *Prophet of Community: The Romantic Socialism of Gustav Landauer* Berkeley: University of California Press

Lyotard, J-F 1984 *The Postmodern Condition: A Report on Knowledge* Manchester: Manchester University Press

McKay, I. 2007 Murray Bookchin (1921-2006) *Anarcho-Syndicalist Review 46*: 39 2014 Libertarian Socialism: Beyond Anarchism and Marxism? *Anarcho-Syndicalist Review 62*: 33-35

McLaughlin, P. 2002 *Michael Bakunin: The Philosophical Basis of His Anarchism* New York: Algora Polishing

McQuinn, J. 2000 *John Clark's Spook: A Critical Review of Max Stirner's Anarchism* Anarchy 68: 54-64

Marshall, P. 1992 *Demanding the Impossible: A History of Anarchism* (revised edition 2008) London: Harper Collins

Marx, K. and F. Engels 1968 *Selected Works* London: Lawrence and Wishart

Maximoff, G.F. (ed) 1953 *The Political Philosophy of Bakunin's Scientific Anarchism* New York: Free Press

May, T. 1994 *The Political Philosophy of Poststructuralist Anarchism* University Park: University of Pennsylvania Press New York: Free Press 2018 Anarchism, Poststructuralism, and Contemporary European Philosophy in N.Jun (ed) *Companion to Anarchism and Philosophy* Leiden: Brill pp 318-339

Meltzer, A. 1996 *I Couldn't Paint Golden* Angels Edinburgh: AK Press

Milliband, R. 1991 *Divided Societies: Class Struggle in Contemporary Capitalism* Oxford: Oxford University Press

Milstein, C. 2010 *Anarchism and its Aspirations* Oakland Ca. AK Press

Molyneux, T. 2011 *Anarchism: A Marxist Critique* London: Bookmarks

Morland, D. 2004 Anti-Capitalism and Poststructuralist Anarchism in J.Purkis and J.Bowen (eds) *Changing Anarchism: Anarchist Theory of Practice in a Global Age* Manchester: Manchester University Press pp 23-38

Morris. B. 1996 *Ecology and Anarchism: Essays and Reviews on Contemporary Thought* Malvern Wells: Images 2004 *Kropotkin: The Politics of Community* Amherst, NY: Humanity Books 2006 *Religion and Anthropology: A Critical Introduction* Cambridge: Cambridge University Press 2014A *Anthropology and the Human Subject* Bloomington: Trafford 2014B *Anthropology, Ecology and Anarchism: A Reader* Oakland, Ca: PM

Press 2014C Bakunin and the Human Subject *Anarchist Studies 22/2*: 8-16 2018 *Visions of Freedom: Critical Writings on Ecology and Anarchism* Montreal: Black Rose Books

Nettlau, M. 1996 *A Short History of Anarchism* London: Freedom Press

Newman, S. 2001 *From Bakunin to Lacan: Anti-Authoritarianism and the Dislocation of Power* New York: Rowman and Littlefield 2004 Anarchism and the Politics of Ressentiment in J.Moore (ed) *I am not a man, I am dynamite* New York: Automedia pp 107-126 2016 *Postanarchism* Cambridge: Polity

Padel, F. and S. Das 2010 *Out of This Earth: East India Adivasis and the Aluminium Cartel* Hyderabad: Orient Blackswan

Parker, S.E et al 2011 *Enemies of Society: an Anthology of Individualist and Egoist Thought* Canada : Ardent Press

Patton, P. 2000 *Deleuze and the Political* London: Routledge

Peacott, J. 1991 *Individualism Reconsidered* Boston: Bad Press

Peck, J. (ed) 1987 *The Chomsky Reader* New York: Panthean

Perlman, F. 1983 *Against His-Story: Against Leviathan* Detroit: Red and Black

Prichard, A. et al (ed) 2017 *Libertarian Socialism: Politics in Red and Black* (original 2012) Oakland, Ca: PM Press

Purkis, J. and J. Bower (eds) 1997 *Twenty-First Century Anarchism* London: Cassell

Rand, A. 1967 *Capitalism: The Unknown Ideal* New York: New American Library

Rapp, J. A. 2012 *Daoism and Anarchism: Critique of State Autonomy in Ancient and Modern China* London: Continuum

Reclus, E. 1903 *Primitive Folk: Studies in Contemporary Ethnology* London: Scott

Rexroth, K. 1975 *Communalism From its Origins to the Twentieth Century* London: Owen

Richards, G. 1982 *The Philosophy of Gandhi* London: Curzon Press

Richards, V. (ed) 2015 *Life and Ideas: The Anarchist Writings of Errico Malatesta* (original 1965) Oakland, CA. PM Press

140

Richardson, J. 2004 *Nietzsche's New Darwinism* Oxford: Oxford University Press

Ricoveri, G. 2013 *Nature for Sale: The Commons versus Commodities* London: Pluto Press

Ritter, A. 1980 *Anarchism: A Theoretical Analysis* Cambridge: Cambridge University Press

Rocker, R. 1989 *Anarcho-Syndicalism* (original 1935) Introd. N.Walter London: Pluto Press

Rorty, R. 1989 *Contingency, Irony and Solidarity* Cambridge: Cambridge University Press

Rouselle, D. and S. Evren (eds) 2011 *Post-Anarchism: A Reader* London: Pluto Press

Seeland, K. (ed) 1997 *Nature is Culture: Indigenous Knowledge and Some Cultural Aspects of Trees* London: Intermediate Technology

Shatz, M. (ed) 1971 *The Essential Works of Anarchism* New York: Bantom Books

Sheehan, S. 2003 *Anarchism* London: Reaktion Books

Sheppard, B.O. 2003 *Anarchism vs Primitivism* Tucson: See Sharp Press

Shone, S.J. 2014 *American Anarchism* Chicago: Haymarket Books

Sim, S. (ed) 2005 *The Routledge Companion to Postmodernism* London: Routledge

Singer, P. 1999 *The Darwinian Left* London: Weidenfeld and Nicholson

Stirner, M. 1973 *The Ego and His Own: The Case of the Individual Against Authority* (original 1845) New York: Dover 2012 *Stirner's Critics* Oakland, Ca. CAL Press

Thomas, E. 1980 *Louise Michel* Montreal: Black Rose Books

Tolstoy, L. 1990 *Government is Violence: Essays on Anarchism and Pacifism* Ed. D. Stephens London: Phoenix Press 1991 *What is to be Done?* (original 1886) Bideford: Green Books

Tormey, S. 2004 *Anti-Capitalism: a Beginners Guide* Oxford: One World Publications

Tucker, B.R. 1972 *Instead of a Book* (original 1893) New York: Arne Press

Turcato, D. (ed) 2014 *The Method of Freedom: A Errico Malatesta Reader* Oakland, Ca. AK Press 2015 *Making Sense of Anarchism: Errico Malatesta's Experiments with Revolution* 1885-1900 Oakland, Ca. AKPress

Van Der Walt, L. and M. Schmidt 2009 *Black Flame: The Revolutionary Class Politics of Anarchism and Syndicalism* Oakland, Ca. AK Press

Vodovnik, Z. 2013 *A Living Spirit of Revolt: The Intrapolitics of Anarchism* Oakland, Ca. PM Press

Walter, N. 2007 *The Anarchist Past and Other Essays* (Ed. D. Goodway) Nottingham: Five Leaves Publications

Ward, C. 1973 *Anarchy in Action* London: Allen and Unwin

Wood, E.M. and J.B. Foster (ed) 1997 *In Defence of History: Marxism and the Postmodern Agenda* New York: Monthly Review Press

Woodcock, G. 1962 *Anarchism: a History of Libertarian Ideas and Movements* London: Penguin Books

Woolgar, S. 1986 On the Alleged Distinction between Discourse and Practice *Social Studies in Science* *16*: 307-317

Young, D.D. 2013 *Against Everything That Is* in H.J. Ehrlich and A.H.S. Boy (eds) *The Best of Social Anarchism* Tucson: see Sharp Press

Zerzan, J. 1994 *Future Primitive and Other Essays* Brooklyn NY: Automedia

Anarchism And The State

by Peter Kropotkin

Across three essays, political philosopher Peter Kropotkin attemptsd to distil his insights into brief but brilliant essays on The State, Anarchism and the ideology for which he became a founding name.

£6 | 100pp | ISBN: 979-1-904491-26-2

The Slow Burning Fuse

by John Quail

John Quail's history of the anarchist movement in Britain from the 1880s-1930s offers unique insights into a force that fascinated, horrified and helped change the face of modern Britain. This new edition features updated foreword & biographies..

£13 | 404pp | ISBN: 978-1-904491-27-9